The Practical Guide to Achieving Customer Satisfaction in Events and Hotels

The Practical Guide to Achieving Customer Satisfaction in Events and Hotels is the fourth title in the Routledge Series *The Practical Guide to Events and Hotel Management* and presents expert-led insight of customer service best practice within events and hotels.

Typical to the other titles in the series, this latest book is written in a logical format and contains practical tips drawn from real-life industry examples, case studies, industry leaders, and the authors' extensive backgrounds working in events and hotel management. Topics include definitions of customer service, an answer to that question 'Is the customer always right?', how to deal with complaints, how to empower staff to recover customer service, and how to turn new customers into loyal customers.

This book is ideal for students of the management of events, hotels, hospitality, or tourism, to be used as a practical resource alongside existing theoretical textbooks. It is also an essential tool for anybody working in the customer-facing industries.

Philip Berners leads the BA Honours Events Management programmes at the Edge Hotel School, University of Essex, UK. Philip has organised every genre of event in the UK, Italy, Portugal, and Poland; he has been the head of events at Thorpe Park, the London Hippodrome, and Camden Palace; and he has been the inhouse event manager for corporations including the Daily Mail Group. Philip's doctorate is in how an events industry takes shape – a study of the UK and Poland. He is a Fellow of the Higher Education Academy and a founding Trustee of the Colchester Museums Development Foundation.

Adrian Martin graduated with a Degree and Masters in Hotel and Catering Management from Manchester University before working for Thistle Hotels in London, Bath, Bristol, and Bedford. He has won two national teaching awards and is currently Vice Principal of the Edge Hotel School at the University of Essex, which he has led to achieve 100% student satisfaction in the National Student Survey. Adrian is researching customer behaviour in restaurants for his PhD.

The Practical Guide to Events and Hotel Management Series

Series Editor: Philip Berners, Edge Hotel School, University of Essex, UK

The Practical Guide to Organising Events
Philip Berners

The Practical Guide to Managing Event Venues
Philip Berners

The Practical Guide to Understanding and Raising Hotel Profitability
Adrian Martin

The Practical Guide to Achieving Customer Satisfaction in Events and Hotels
Philip Berners and Adrian Martin

For more information about this series, please visit: https://www.routledge.com/tourism/series/PGE

The Practical Guide to Achieving Customer Satisfaction in Events and Hotels

Philip Berners and Adrian Martin

Routledge
Taylor & Francis Group

LONDON AND NEW YORK

Cover image: Valencia Conference Centre

First published 2023
by Routledge
4 Park Square, Milton Park, Abingdon, Oxon OX14 4RN

and by Routledge
605 Third Avenue, New York, NY 10158

Routledge is an imprint of the Taylor & Francis Group, an informa business

British Library Cataloguing-in-Publication Data
A catalogue record for this book is available from the British Library

Library of Congress Cataloging-in-Publication Data
Names: Berners, Philip, author. | Martin, Adrian, author.
Title: The practical guide to achieving customer satisfaction in events and hotels / Philip Berners and Adrian Martin.
Description: Abingdon, Oxon; New York, NY: Routledge, 2022. | Series: Practical guide events hotel management | Includes bibliographical references and index.
Subjects: LCSH: Hospitality industry—Customer services. | Hotel management. | Special events—Management.
Classification: LCC TX911.3.C8 B47 2022 (print) | LCC TX911.3.C8 (ebook) | DDC 647.94068—dc23/eng/20220422
LC record available at https://lccn.loc.gov/2022001392
LC ebook record available at https://lccn.loc.gov/2022001393

ISBN: 978-0-367-72387-3 (hbk)
ISBN: 978-0-367-72385-9 (pbk)
ISBN: 978-1-003-15460-0 (ebk)

DOI: 10.4324/9781003154600

Typeset in Iowan Old Style
by codeMantra

This book is dedicated to the memory of Ambassador Dr Ryszard Żółtaniecki (1951–2020), professor, sociologist, diplomat, poet, friend.

Contents

List of Figures	*x*
List of Tables	*xi*
Note from the Series Editor	*xii*
Acknowledgements	*xiv*

Introduction	**1**
1 What Is Customer Satisfaction?	**3**
1.0 Defining Customer Satisfaction	3
1.1 The Dangers of Overselling and Underselling	7
1.2 The Customer Journey	15
1.3 Total Quality Management	23
1.4 Service Quality Management (SERVQUAL)	27
1.5 Customer Balanced Scorecard	28
2 Why Is Customer Satisfaction Important?	**30**
2.0 The Value of Reputation	43
2.1 The Cost of Not Achieving Customer Satisfaction	49
3 Knowing Your Customers	**52**
3.0 Knowing Your Competition	53
3.1 Knowing Your Target Market	55
3.2 Personalising Your Offer	57
3.3 Customer Relationship Management	60

3.4 Customer Loyalty   61

3.5 Customer Referrals   62

4   Know Your Promise to the Customer   **65**

4.0 Is the Customer Always Right?   66

4.1 What Can You Deliver?   68

4.2 Setting Customer Expectations   70

4.3 Customer Perception of Hotels   74

     4.3.1 Hotel Brands   75

     4.3.2 Hotel Marketing Consortia   77

     4.3.3 Star Rating   78

     4.3.4 Online Review Sites/OTAs/Online Booking Sites   78

     4.3.5 Hotel Accreditation   80

4.4 Events   80

     4.4.1 Setting Event Objectives   84

5   Contracts   **89**

5.0 Confirming the Promise with Contracts   89

6   Improving Customer Loyalty   **97**

6.0 Repeat Customers   98

6.1 At Leadership Level   101

6.2 At Management Level   105

6.3 At Operational Level   107

     6.3.1 Underperforming Staff   109

6.4 The Communication Process   111

     6.4.1 Effective Communication   113

     6.4.2 Hotel Interdepartmental Communication   115

     6.4.3 Hotel Interdepartmental Consistency of Performance   116

     6.4.4 Event Interdepartmental Communication   118

     6.4.5 Departmental Communication   122

7   Dealing with Complaints   **123**

7.0 Why Customers Complain   124

7.1 Legislation of Complaints   125

7.2 Types of Complainers   126

7.3 Transactional Analysis – A Psychological Technique to Deal with Difficult Customers   127

7.4 Handling Legitimate Complaints 129

7.5 The Eight-Step Method to Dealing with Complaints 132

7.6 Complaints at Events 137

7.7 Negotiating a Resolution 138

7.8 Possible Complaint Outcomes 140

7.9 Case Study Examples of Actual Complaints from the Event Industry 140

    7.9.1 Case Study 1 – Uncooked Chicken Served at a Wedding 140

    7.9.2 Case Study 2 – Steak Preferences at a Conference 144

8 Empowering Staff to Resolve Customer Service Issues 146

8.0 The Benefits 146

8.1 The Benefits for Staff 150

8.2 The Benefits for Management 150

8.3 The Benefits for Customers 151

8.4 The Benefits for the Business 153

8.5 Servant Leadership to Increase Employee and Customer Satisfaction 155

    8.5.1 Servant Leadership – Employee Satisfaction 159

    8.5.2 Servant Leadership – Customer Satisfaction 160

    8.5.3 The Service-Profit Chain 162

9 The Importance of Reflection 165

9.0 The Benefit of Reflection 165

9.1 Reflecting in the Customer Perspective 166

9.2 Well, Would You Complain? 168

Index *175*

Figures

1.1	Fluctuation in Quality	10
1.2	Flattening the Quality Line	10
1.3	Customer Expectations of Quality 1	11
1.4	Customer Expectations of Quality 2	11
1.5	Driving Quality Upwards	11
1.6	Touch Points	18
1.7	Error Rate of Touch Points	21
1.8	SERVQUAL Model	28
1.9	Balanced Scorecard	29
3.1	Competitor Analysis Scatter Graph	54
3.2	Fictional Customer Persona	56
3.3	Percentage Source of Bookings	63
6.1	Upward Spiral of Success	101
6.2	The Shannon & Weaver Model of Communication	111
6.3	Cutlip & Center's 7 Cs of Effective Communication	113
7.1	Transactional Analysis Matching Series	128
8.1	Traditional Leadership Hierarchy Challenges	157
8.2	Servant Leadership Hierarchy	158
8.3	The Service-Profit Chain (SPC)	162
9.1	Management Model of Reflection	166
9.2	Kolb's Experiential Learning Cycle	167
9.3	Customer Service Appraisal	170
9.4	Service Appraisal Template	171
9.5	Event Function Sheet	171

Tables

1.1 Using Staff Feedback Revisit the List of Touch Points One by One   20
7.1 Categorisation and Tracking of Complaint Outcomes   141

Note from the Series Editor

I created the Routledge book series *The Practical Guide to Events and Hotel Management* after transitioning into teaching from a career in hospitality and events management. In the forum of classrooms and lecture theatres, I realised there was a lack of practical know-how within the theoretical academic textbooks available to students. Well, that would be fine if this were law or history and required an abundance of theory. But students of events management and hotel management choose a university course to learn more about how to do the job and are less interested in theoretical texts.

This is why the books in this series are written in a logical and readable format and style, packed with industry knowledge and tips drawn from real-life practical experience to provide a supportive resource to existing theoretical literature.

The books in this series are also designed for those who are already working in the event and hotel industries and might need a guidebook on how to do it right, without the need to attend a class or be under the tutelage of a university lecturer.

The Practical Guide to Organising Events

The first book in this series is structured around the key stages of event management – pre-event, during-event, and post-event. It offers essential practical insights and guidance throughout the whole process of managing an event. Topics covered include proposal writing, event planning, budgeting, funding and sponsorship, health and safety, risk management, security, and event evaluation.

The Practical Guide to Managing Event Venues

The second book in this series focuses on venues for events. It covers developing the client relationship, marketing of venues, financial accountability, risk planning, interdepartmental communication, onsite procedures, and post-event evaluation.

The Practical Guide to Understanding and Raising Profits in Hotels

The third book in the series is authored by Adrian Martin who is Vice Principal of the Edge Hotel School, University of Essex and a respected lecturer of hotel management subjects. This book is a written form of Adrian's teaching and will assist in understanding the fundamental need to achieve profit and how to do so.

The Practical Guide to Achieving Customer Satisfaction in Events and Hotels

The fourth title in this series brings events and hotels into one book to deal with everything about customer service. The book aims to guide managers to achieve complete customer service and uphold the highest level of customer service standards. The topics include how to set customer expectations, dealing with customer complaints, why customers complain, empowering staff to recover customer service, the value of customer evaluation and feedback, and knowing what you are promising your customers.

Philip Berners, Series Editor
London, 2022

Acknowledgements

The authors would like to thank the following contributors for providing their industry insights into customer service, which are shown in the 'Industry Voice' boxes throughout this book:

- Sally Beck, General Manager, Royal Lancaster Hotel, London.

- Oliver Brown, General Manager, Wivenhoe House Hotel, Colchester.

- Andrew Coggings, Managing Director of Hospitality, The Goodwood Estate.

- David Connell, General Manager, South Lodge Hotel, Horsham.

- Dan Gatehouse, General Manager, Victorian House Hotel, Grasmere.

- Rak Kalidas, Commercial Director, Levy UK.

- Olaf Olenski, Customer Service Expert, formerly at Harrods of Knightsbridge.

- Danny Pecorelli, Managing Director, Exclusive Collection.

- Adam Rowledge, Managing Director, Rowledge Associates.

- James Young, Head of Events, Colchester Events Company.

We also thank the team at Routledge for their continued support during the production of this book: Harriet Cunningham, Carlotta Fanton, and Emma Travis.

Introduction

This book provides a practical guide to achieving customer satisfaction at events and hotels because all managers want their customers to be happy but it is a difficult aim to achieve.

Typical to the Routledge series, *The Practical Guide to Events and Hotel Management*, this book is written in a logical, readable, and easy-to-follow style with author and industry anecdotes and case studies as examples to what is being explained. The book provides a no-nonsense tool for students of events, hotel, hospitality, leisure, and tourism management. But it is written also for those who are already working in these industries and would like to learn more about how to achieve excellent customer service.

Chapter 1 defines customer satisfaction and how important it is to set customer expectations which are not too high or low for the offer being provided to customers. We look at how customers journey through your services and then we visit some of the models of customer service such as Total Quality Management (TQM), Service Quality Management (SERVQUAL), and the Customer Balanced Scorecard.

Chapter 2 leads with the understanding of why customer service is important to provide and uphold, what it means to the reputation of an event or a hotel, and what the cost will be if customers do not receive the service they expect.

DOI: 10.4324/9781003154600-1

Chapter 3 discusses knowing your customers, your competitors, and the target markets for the services you offer to customers. We visit the benefits of personalising that offer to your customers, developing the customer relationship, and the value of using a computerised Customer Relationship Management (CRM) system. This chapter also covers customer loyalty and how to convert new customers to be loyal customers, and the need for customer referrals.

Chapter 4 considers what you promise your customers and investigates whether there is truth in the idiom 'the customer is always right'. We look at knowing what you are capable to deliver to customers and how to manage customer expectations. Exploring the area of customer expectations takes us into the perception of hotels through their use of brands, marketing consortia, the star rating system, online booking systems and review sites, and hotel accreditation bodies. We then move into the events arena and discuss the value of setting event objectives.

Chapter 5 explains the need for contracts to confirm the promise being made to customers for the services you are offering and which the customer expects to receive.

Chapter 6 leads the way through customer loyalty – how to improve loyalty from customers and retain repeat customers. We discuss this topic from the three perspectives of leadership, management, and operation, and we look at how to deal with staff who are underperforming. With managing people, we have to look at communication processes and we do this by breaking it down into hotel department and inter-department communications and then events communications describing the tools for communication across the team and wider stakeholders, including production meetings, pre-event briefings, and onsite briefings.

Chapter 7 explains how to deal with complaints and why customers complain. We present a typology of complainers, the need to identify the legitimacy of a complaint to know what to offer to resolve it, and we provide an eight-step method to deal with complaints. In this chapter, we look at complaints specific to events, negotiating resolutions and possible complaint outcomes. There are two case study examples of real-life complaints at events.

Chapter 8 investigates the benefits of empowering staff to deal with complaints and recover customer service levels. We take you, in turn, through the benefits for staff, managers, customers, and the business.

Chapter 9 points out the importance of reflection and what benefits it provides to stop and reflect. We view this from the customer perspective and then ask, 'well, would you complain?'

Chapter **1**

What Is Customer Satisfaction?

1.0 Defining Customer Satisfaction

This chapter sets out to define customer service and customer satisfaction by identifying events and hotels as providing a service to customers. We identify the difference between a product and providing a service and why a service is difficult to recover if it goes wrong.

Section 1.1 looks at meeting customer expectations and the dangers of overselling or underselling and being dishonest about what the customer can expect to receive.

In Section 1.2, we track the 'customer journey' where we look at how customers use 'touch points' when utilising event and hotel services. We explore varied sources of customer expectations and discuss stakeholders and stakeholder groups.

Section 1.3 explains the merits of providing Total Quality Management (TQM) drawing upon various hotel and event examples including planned maintenance versus repairs to equipment which has already failed.

Section 1.4 introduces the SERVQUAL service quality management model using the gap analysis technique.

DOI: 10.4324/9781003154600-2

Section 1.5 shows the Balanced Scorecard model to measure performance beyond profit only.

Events and hotels provide a service because the product for customers is both provided and consumed simultaneously.

When an attendee to an event arrives at the venue, the service is delivered at that point. The event begins with the arrival of guests. Entering through the doors, the guest is greeted or received through security, guest lists, lanyards, or wristbands. Once inside the event, the customer goes to the cloakroom, the bar, the restaurant or buffet, or the dancefloor – each service they receive is delivered at the point of being consumed until they leave the venue.

When a hotel guest checks-in, the services are delivered at that point, beginning at reception, the check-in, entering their bedroom, ordering room service, visiting the restaurant, and the bar – right through the customer journey until they check out.

What the customer perceives of the services you provide is customer service.

Customer service does not end when the customer leaves the venue or checks-out of their hotel. It can continue after the customer has departed. Good customer service tracks the customer after they leave by engaging with them on social media platforms or direct contacts through emails or letter in the form of promotions for future offers and customer survey feedback questionnaires.

The issue with providing a service – that is, where the service is delivered and consumed at the same point – is that it cannot be easily recovered if something goes wrong. If a customer is dissatisfied with any part of the service they receive, they are already consuming it. This is why live events and hotel bedrooms are considered as 'perishable' because once a live event ends or the night has been spent in a hotel, it cannot rehappen. It has been consumed. An event which happens tonight cannot be consumed tomorrow night, and a hotel room available on the 12th June cannot again be sold on that date, that is, the 12th June.

This means that if customer service is not right at the event or in the hotel, it cannot be put right afterwards.

The emphasis, then, must be to ensure that customer service is right in the first place and that each customer receives the service they expected to receive from the perception given to them by the event or the hotel.

The emphasis here is in getting it right. If a customer purchases a product in a store and is dissatisfied with that product, they can return it, exchange it, or receive a refund for it. These actions cause little inconvenience for the customer. The customer may experience mild disappointment and a modicum of inconvenience but it is unlikely to ruin their day, their enjoyment, their experience, their trip, or their holiday.

It is different when purchasing a service to be received. When a customer travels to an event or hotel, any failure in customer service will cause a higher level of disappointment and a great deal of inconvenience. They have decided to make a purchase based on an anticipated expectation of what they will receive at a future point. The customer has planned and prepared in readiness for the event or trip. They will spend time by travelling to get to the event or hotel and spend further time at that event or hotel consuming the service.

It can be seen that any failure in their enjoyment of their purchase will have psychological impacts on top of financial and social impacts.

One of the problems is consumer behaviour in decision-making. Once a customer has evaluated the decision and decided to make a purchase (to attend an event or stay in a hotel), then there is a time lag between the point of purchase and the date of the event or their stay in the hotel. This lag between purchase and visit causes post-purchase behaviour.

During the lag, the customer builds their anticipation leading up to the event or their stay in a hotel. They will plan for it and build their excitement towards it. They might tell their friends and family about where they are going and bring other people into the expectation and anticipation, all the whilst upwardly constructing their expectations of the experience they will receive. The customer will perhaps make advanced preparations to be at the event or hotel such as arranging child-minding, dog-sitting, house-sitting, plus their own preparations of packing to travel and selecting what to wear.

Then comes the experience itself – the day of the event or their stay in the hotel. By this time they have heightened their expectation of their enjoyment of the experience. The customer certainly expects at least to receive what was promised when they made the decision to purchase.

After receiving the experience, the customer adopts post-experience behaviour. If their experience at the point of consumption of the service they receive falls below their heightened expectations, they will then adopt a negative post-experience attitude. In this attitude, customers will abandon the event or hotel by never returning and will spread negative word of mouth. All the people who were involved in the expectation and anticipation will now be informed of the failures and disappointments, and it will likely be exaggerated to justify how the customer feels.

Unless the customer complains to the event or hotel, The Manager will not be aware of the customer's abandonment or that they are spreading negative word of mouth. The Manager will also not know what the customer is saying and why (so The Manager cannot learn from this), and The Manager cannot correct or control the customer's negative attitude and post-experience behaviour.

If the customer receives good customer service at the event or hotel and they enjoy the experience because it meets or exceeds their expectations, the customer adopts a positive post-experience attitude and will exhibit behaviours such as repeat attendance, positive word of mouth, and the purchase of associated products such as merchandise.

When measuring and defining 'customer satisfaction', there is tendency to focus only on the quality of the service being received by the consumer.

However, satisfaction is a comparison of the quality of the service received versus the quality the consumer was expecting.

For instance, an exclusive event in the ballroom of a five-star hotel immediately raises expectations which would not be satisfied by an average event experience. Alternatively, a customer being sold a ticket to a budget event in a venue which from the outside looks low quality, may be pleasantly surprised and satisfied with even just an average event experience.

Customer Perception + Customer Expectation = Customer Satisfaction (CP + CE = CS)

INDUSTRY VOICE

"Employees are far less likely to be customer focused if their employer is not employee focused.

As an operator, by putting your people first and creating a quality employee experience and strong culture, team members will exhibit higher levels of motivation to deliver the best possible customer experience, but also to drive other key factors such as profitability.

An employee-centric business that recruits the right people and creates the right environment in which they can succeed is key to motivating employees to be customer focused".

Adam Rowledge, Managing Director, Rowledge Associates

Customer satisfaction can therefore be defined as the measure of the difference between the customer's expectations and the perception of the experience they received. The question is, does their perception of the service quality they received meet with what they *expected* to receive?

If the measure is positive, customers will be satisfied, maybe even delighted. If the measure is negative, the customer will be dissatisfied and may complain or spread negative feedback about the business.

There are two distinct aspects to achieving customer satisfaction:

One is about communicating the right message about your event or hotel, sharing what it will genuinely look like to the attendee or guest, and avoiding overpromising to the customer so that realistic expectations are set.

The other is about ensuring what was promised is delivered in a consistent manner to every customer.

Both aspects need to come together to achieve 100% customer satisfaction.

There are several variables discussed throughout this book that can work against events and hotels, which will prevent the achievement of 100% customer satisfaction.

1.1 The Dangers of Overselling and Underselling

It is natural for an event manager or hotel manager – from hereon we refer to both as 'The Manager' – to aspire to deliver the best possible experience to event attendees and hotel guests. This is why some managers make promises which cannot always be delivered. The best intent may be there, but the service that was promised cannot always be delivered – this is overselling. The problem with this is that it raises the expectations of the customer who believes they are going to receive what was promised, but in actuality they will not.

Overselling occurs naturally and often because The Manager genuinely does want to deliver what they promise to their customers and intends to deliver it. They might also genuinely believe that they are delivering that promise. Also, customers want to believe that they are going to receive the best and will not question that the promise might fall short (until it does).

This is where the relationship between the marketing department and The Manager can be interesting. The Manager sets the financial sales targets and relies heavily on the marketing department to bring in the right amount of business to meet those statistics.

The Manager also relies on the marketing department to bring in the right type of business. This requires honesty. Honesty from The Manager in knowing what type of business suits the event or hotel; honesty with targeting the right markets;

honesty with the level of service they provide; and honesty with the customers so that their expectations match the experience they will receive.

Let us be clear on this point. Dishonesty does not win customers for the long term. It wins people who attend an event or visit a hotel but will leave disappointed. This does not make them customers – it makes them fools for believing the lie.

Customers do know what they expect from the event or hotel and if it does not match – if there was dishonesty somewhere in the chain of perception – they will feel cheated. They might complain, demand refunds or discounts, or they might say nothing but never provide return business. They might even tell everyone they know, not to attend that event or visit that hotel. We do that, don't we?

That question – 'we do that, don't we' – is for you to think about for a moment. You have been a customer, haven't you? You are a customer today. You will be a customer tomorrow. So, as The Manager who is in control of what customers are receiving, you must think about how you would feel and react if a service you had paid for does not live up to your expectations. And if your perception of that expectation was provided to you by that very event or hotel, you will be upset or angry. You will feel cheated as a customer, just like your customers will feel. You might complain, demand a refund or discount, or you might say nothing but vow never to return to that event or hotel. You might even tell everyone you know not to attend that event or visit that hotel. Yes, we do that, don't we?

At the outset here, we can appreciate that customers are ourselves and we are all the same. We all want to receive the service we expected to receive. If something is promised to us, we expect that promise to be delivered otherwise we know it is not right. We all dislike dishonesty and being cheated. We will want to do something about it if something is not right with the experience of the service we receive.

It is easy for The Manager to put themselves in the position of their customers: the 'customer perspective'.

Back to honesty, then. Customer expectations can be lifted by marketing, sometimes beyond what can be delivered, which is the overselling part. There are always limitations with what can be delivered – be honest about that. Limitations might include a lack of staff or shortage of stock. It might be the level of service that can be provided at that time. But the time and energy spent dealing with complaints due to underdelivering to customers' heightened expectations; their refusals to pay; having to compromise profit by issuing refunds; the negative publicity on review websites; and long-term damage to the reputation of the event or hotel far outweigh the short-term sales boost achieved from raising customer expectations beyond what can be delivered.

AUTHOR'S VOICE

This is an example of poor customer perspective:

I recently attended an event at a four-star country house hotel and I wanted to visit the restroom. I walked through reception and the lounge areas but could not find the restroom or any signs to indicate where they are located. I was therefore forced to wait in line at reception and then ask for the location of the restrooms which happen to be on the lower ground floor. How would I know that?

Now, I do not think it is right for me to have to announce that I am visiting the toilet, or be placed in the situation where I feel that I am asking permission to go to the toilet! So why are the restrooms not clearly signposted and easy to locate? Why must every guest who is unfamiliar with that hotel find it necessary to walk around looking for the restrooms and then have to ask a member of staff where they are? Why are they hidden; why is it a secret?

Okay, the inconvenience was mild, but the issue here is that most guests will wish to visit the restrooms in a venue, so this scenario must occur frequently, and the staff must get asked the same question repeatedly. Yet, The Manager has not identified this problem, and if they have, why have they not done anything about it? Maybe they have overlooked the customer service experience their guests receive.

Whatever it is, they failed to put themselves in the perspective of their customers because if they had, they would not like that service, either.

It is the job of The Manager to maintain consistent standards. And it is the job of the marketing department to sell the product they are delivering, in the most effective way possible, but within the boundaries of what can be delivered consistently.

A theory developed by one of the authors of this book displays this as a graphic in Figure 1.1.

If *time* is the x-axis and *quality* is the y-axis, it can be seen that the level of quality in this particular event venue fluctuates daily, weekly, and maybe even hourly.

The critical job of The Manager is to not only improve the quality of the event or hotel but also the consistency of the services it delivers to customers. This

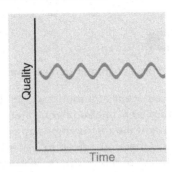

Figure 1.1 Fluctuation in Quality

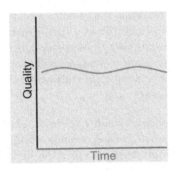

Figure 1.2 Flattening the Quality Line

would mean both raising and flattening the quality line (see Figure 1.2) so that the customer receives a consistent service and it is not up-and-down depending on all sorts of variables.

In direct contrast to this, the job of the marketing manager is to drive sales and revenue upwards – that is, the number of tickets sold as well as the average price. An over-enthusiastic marketing manager might push customer expectations too high with both an unrealistic message and too high a price. This would create expectations of customers (represented by individual dots on the graph in Figure 1.3) above anything The Manager could deliver.

If The Manager is unsuccessful in raising quality and consistency, there will be times when the expectations of the customer are beyond what has been delivered (represented by B points in Figure 1.4) as well as times when customer expectations are exceeded (points A in Figure 1.4).

If The Manager and the marketing manager are closely aligned with a consistent quality and realistic messaging at the right price, then the expectations of

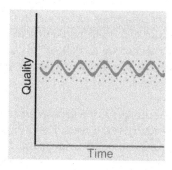

Figure 1.3 Customer Expectations of Quality 1

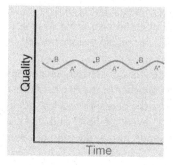

Figure 1.4 Customer Expectations of Quality 2

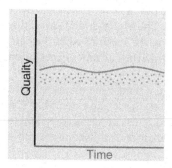

Figure 1.5 Driving Quality Upwards

customers will always be met. Therefore, the job of the marketing manager is to sell as many tickets (events) or rooms (hotels) as possible without raising expectations beyond the quality line, whilst The Manager drives up the quality to enable even more sales (Figure 1.5).

Overselling is a familiar but dangerous technique. But The Manager may decide to perform underselling and task their marketing manager with purposefully underselling an event as a technique to 'delight' customers. In which case customers will arrive to the event with low expectations and be delighted with the unexpected quality they receive.

This is a useful marketing technique as it will push the customer to broadcast their experience and essentially advertise the event. Positive word of mouth is powerful and can be worth the reduced income of having reduced sales at a low price.

Underselling can be as dangerous as overselling, however. Marketing a lower perception to customers can devalue an event or a hotel. It can determine lower pricing points so that the cost of a ticket to an event or the price of a hotel room aligns with the marketing message being undersold. This would have financial impacts on the business but could also drive away potential customers who believe it is a lower quality, lower priced event or hotel.

Price is one of the key indicators of setting perceptions because a customer can measure one price against another in the marketplace and arrive at a judgement. A low price point could give the perception of low quality, whereas a higher price point can add value to the event or hotel and make it seem more worthwhile which would influence the purchasing decision of the customer.

Where overselling (promising more than the customer might receive) and underselling (attracting customers by a lower price point) are techniques being considered, great care must be taken to keep within the parameters of honesty. The boundaries can be flexible but not over-reached to become dishonest. When employing these techniques, The Manager and marketing department must know how far they are stretching the truth of what they are promising the customer and are able to deliver within the customer expectations being set.

There are occasions where a marketing manager may have mis-sold events and raised customer expectations to such an extent that The Manager cannot possibly deliver the quality required. This can cause complaints and can even result in litigation because misrepresentation is a dishonest act covered by trading standards.

Dealing with the general public as customers has positive and negative aspects. This is what makes the hospitality and events industry diverse and exciting because each customer is unique. Anyone in the role of pleasing their customers – event managers and hotel managers, of course – has a social, legal, and professional responsibility to keep their customers happy. This is why people become event managers and hotel managers – they like to be able to keep their customers happy. That is the satisfaction of the job, and happy customers are the reward for a job done well.

AUTHOR'S VOICE

In November 2008, two brothers tricked thousands of customers into visiting their 'Lapland New Forest' attraction by promoting it as a winter wonderland theme park with snow-covered log cabins, a nativity scene, husky dogs, polar bears, and a bustling Christmas market.

Visitors were charged £30 per ticket, and with up to 10,000 advance bookings online for a range of tickets including family purchases, the brothers were set to gross over £1.2 million.

In reality, disappointed families arrived to a muddy field with a broken ice rink, and fairy lights strung from trees. Within days there had been hundreds of complaints to trading standards officials, and the attraction had closed.

After Dorset Trading Standards officers prosecuted the brothers, they were found guilty on eight charges of misleading advertising and were fined over £100,000 and jailed for 13 months.

Source: *Daily Mail*

It can present The Manager with extremes of delighted customers as well as angry and disgruntled customers at the same event or in the same hotel. This is because customer expectations can vary from one customer to another from the same marketing message. This is the challenge and should be relished because that is the job of providing good customer service. Challenges present learning opportunities for self-development and professional development. Experience of challenges such as these is valuable for future situations which is why employers look for candidates with experience in customer service. Remember, all experiences arising from challenges are good for the curriculum vitae.

There is a saying that we can only please 95% of customers 95% of the time as a measure of success, rather than 100%.

But should The Manager tolerate such a failure rate? Is this level of unfulfilled expectations inevitable, or can it be managed?

To answer these questions requires an understanding of the breadth of sources of information a customer relies upon when setting their own expectations before arriving to an event or hotel:

- **External communications** – all the advertising and social media communication that has gone out will help shape the customers' expectations. Photoshopped pictures of the best areas of the venue or hotel, for instance, can raise expectations (and sales). The social media output and overall wording of text will create a picture, realistic or otherwise, of the event the customer will experience.

- **Brand reputation** – one of the advantages of a well-respected brand is the pre-conceived expectations it brings to customers. This assists with sales but can raise customers' expectations to unrealistic levels.

- **Word of mouth (WOM)** – customers can exaggerate to an unrealistic level which transfers to become other customers' expectations. This is outside the control of The Manager and is seen as positive in terms of generating sales, but the payoff is in increasing customer expectations beyond what can be delivered.

- **Online reviews** – like word of mouth, but a permanent and public version with some customers willing to exaggerate the positive and the negative. This will again impact other customers.

- **Previous experience** – the customer may have been to this event or hotel previously and have a pre-conceived expectation that it will be as good, if not better, this time around. Human memory is not perfect, and some customers may have a romanticised memory that can be difficult to replicate.

- **Psychology** – some customers are perfectionists and transfer this behaviour trait to their expectations as a consumer. Minor faults that would go unnoticed by most customers are flagged and focused upon by a minority of customers. These customers are practiced at finding errors and can sometimes highlight them at events or in hotels.

- **Perception** – the quality the customer perceives from the event or hotel is somehow not in line with other customers due to the way they perceive the world around them. Some people have a positive outlook and others have a negative outlook, for instance. This will shape their own perceptions of what they are experiencing.

Anyone working in the events or hotel industry will be familiar with the minority of customers who are almost impossible to please. These customers will find fault easily and their expectations are unrealistic and very difficult, if not impossible to satisfy.

The solution would be to lower the messaging imagery and the price so that the expectations of this type of customers are reduced (underselling).

However, the examples above demonstrate that it is not always within the control of The Manager or marketing manager to satisfy every customer, so underselling may not fully resolve the problem. Furthermore, reducing the marketing and price may devalue the product and be financially unviable.

There is an argument, therefore, that pleasing 95% of customers 95% of the time is a sensible and reasonable target to achieve.

Yet, this would mean that only just over 90% of customers are satisfied ($0.95 \times 0.95 = 0.9025$). This does not sound like a stretch target. Surely that minority of customers who are impossible to please account for less than 5% of all customers. And those who are possible to please should be satisfied every time in an elite organisation.

Perhaps the target, therefore, should be pleasing 99% of customers 100% of the time, in partial recognition that maybe 1% of customers are wrong.

INDUSTRY VOICE

"As a developing events business we are very protective of our brand and how it is represented.

Reputation is everything in the events industry and one bad representation can have detrimental effects for a long period of time.

Whilst a wide and varied route to market is required, continuity of brand, image and message is imperative to the success of any company".

James Young, Head of Events, Colchester Events Company

1.2 The Customer Journey

Event and hotel services are complicated and made up of multiple elements, some of which are outside the control of The Manager. For example, levels of traffic on the night of an event cannot be controlled by an event manager. Additionally, there is the diversity of customers to satisfy from leisure guests, corporate clients, special event clientele, VIPs, and press. It can be seen how complicated it is to consistently meet the expectations of all types of customers.

Hotels have diversified their original services to offer event spaces, bars, cafes, restaurants, gymnasium and leisure facilities, in-room dining, lounges, and a range of types of room including suites, executive rooms, business rooms, and family rooms. Then there are sectors within the hotel marketplace which includes star-rated hotels, budget hotels, leisure hotels, resort hotels, convention hotels, city centre hotels, country house hotels, and boutique hotels.

The diversity and range of types of customer and types of hotels require the identification of target markets. The Manager must know and understand the customers in their business to meet the needs and expectations of these individual customer groups – adopting the stakeholder perspective to understand how they think and what they want.

Identifying stakeholder groups – whether customers or clients, or all other stakeholders such as sponsors and suppliers – is essential to understand individual stakeholder groups and identify their needs, wishes, and desires. An event client, for example, may have needs for the event to be profitable and for their invited guests to have a memorable and enjoyable experience, whereas a sponsor providing a bar at the same event may have the need for his product to be visible and for the product to be sampled by guests at the event.

The sponsor has decided to provide a bar and product for the purpose of marketing reach to the audience attending the event. This could be because of the profile of guests that they meet his target drinker demographic and that they are all over 18 and can legally consume alcohol. It could be because there is a charity angle to the event and he would like his product to be associated with that good cause. Or if there are celebrities and press in attendance at the event, he might decide to participate as a sponsor because of the prospect of his product being photographed in the hands of a celebrity.

But the client is interested in different outcomes. Their objective is not the bar product, but the success of the event defined by their objectives (stated above as profit and their guests having a memorable and enjoyable experience). Part of that client objective will be satisfied by the sponsored bar because the sponsor lessens the costs of bar products (meaning more profit) and the donated bar product contributes to guests having that memorable and enjoyable experience. So, in this case, both the client and sponsor objectives get satisfied.

Here, we can see that by identifying the needs and desires of individual stakeholder groups, there is greater likelihood of meeting those needs.

It is usual to use the term 'individual stakeholder *groups*' because stakeholders do fall into groups. Customers, for example, can be identified as an individual group of stakeholders, as can sponsors, and suppliers. But we could further identify individual stakeholders as sub-groups at events and in hotels, and sometimes this is necessary if each stakeholder is specifically different to another or if within each stakeholder group there are individual needs. For example, there could be a range of customers within the customer stakeholder group such as general ticket holders, premium ticket holders, VIP ticket holders, seated ticket holders, standing ticket holders, and balcony ticket holders. The same is true with sponsors – there could be a main (*headline* or *title*) sponsor who has paid a higher cost for a premium sponsorship package which other lesser (*satellite*) sponsors do not receive. So, within various stakeholder groups (such as ticket holders and sponsors in these examples), we may need to identify individual stakeholders to understand their specific needs and desires and meet their expectations.

Each event or hotel is made up of multiple 'touch points' where the customer encounters the business and its services, thereby creating the possibility for errors along the way. Very few services in other industries have as many touch points over such a long period of time, which makes controlling service quality in events and hotels particularly challenging.

The positive way of looking at this is that it also creates an opportunity to outperform competitors in a way that is not possible in many other industries.

Event and hotel businesses that get this right – that are consistent in their offer and maintain high levels of customer satisfaction – hold a special place in the market. For example, the wedding venue which must be booked years in advance to get a booking, or the music festival that sells out of its 203,000 tickets within 36 minutes of going on sale (Glastonbury, 2021).

The first step to achieving total quality is in knowing the product down to the smallest detail. This requires following the customer journey and analysing each step along the way to look for touch points and identify where possible errors might occur.

For instance, a one-off entertainment event with food and drink could create 200 or more touch points, some of which are shown in Figure 1.6 by way of a simplified example.

It is widely reported that when Jean-Marc Gales took over the car manufacturer Lotus, one of the first things he was rumoured to do was pull apart every single piece of their top-selling car. Each of the parts was labelled – over 1,000 of them – and staff were encouraged to find ways to improve and lighten each piece to improve the speed and performance of the car.

This process can be applied to any industry, even service industries, and is used to make incremental improvements.

Following the principle of the Lotus example, an event can be dissected into touch points to identify possible errors and any opportunities to improve the service to the customer.

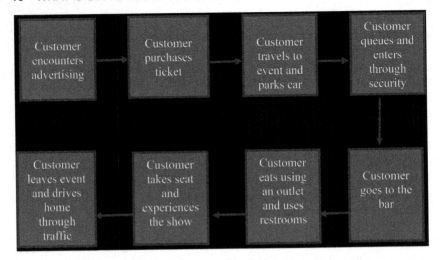

Figure 1.6 Touch Points

INDUSTRY VOICE

"When starting a new role you have only a limited period where you can sense check the current position of the business by asking questions to understand why things are done this way: 'Is there a better way of doing it'; 'What would it take to improve the sales in this area by 20%+'; 'How to save costs in this area?' etc.

There are always quick wins and efficiencies that can be found in all areas of the business, but it takes time and effort.

Not only can this be beneficial to the P&L (profit and loss statement) but is also a great opportunity to get to know your team and develop a strong bond. The team will know so much more about the inefficiencies in their area and by asking the right questions they will give you the answers".

David Connell, General Manager, South Lodge 5star Hotel

To do this it is necessary to take the place of the customer – adopting the customer perspective – and move through the timeline step by step:

Example: Touch Points of a Comedy Show with a Meal:

- Directions to the venue were clear and easy to follow

- On arrival there was parking available close to the main building
- Access to the venue was clear and it was easy to go through security
- The external look of the venue was well maintained
- The lobby had a pleasing ambience and was clean and tidy
- There was no queue at security and for ticket checks
- The welcome host smiled and gave their immediate and undivided attention
- Staff were well-groomed and easy to identify in clean, smart uniform
- Staff spoke in a clear and calm manner
- The booking details were correct without spelling errors
- The booking terms were correct and confirmed
- Staff gave all necessary details for the event and directed you to your table
- You could find the restrooms
- Food arrived in a timely manner and to the right standard
- Drinks could be ordered easily and delivered timely
- The show started on time with clear information on how the entertainment would progress, location of toilets, and break times
- The performers were of a high standard, and the sound was clear and at the right volume
- Instructions on how to leave were clear and safe
- Bills were paid easily and promptly
- There were no queues when leaving
- There was minimal traffic when leaving

If this process is continued throughout the entire customer journey in more depth, it might identify over 100 touch points. This is why consistency is difficult to achieve in events and hotels because the quality of the service will vary not just day by day, but hour by hour.

The next step in the process is to quantify the error rate of each touch point – that is, how often each stage in the customer journey has a fault.

There may be evidence of this from the feedback in surveys, customer comment cards, and online reviews, but it is the staff who are best positioned to provide the answers. It is the staff who will be fixing faults and dealing with complaints

Table 1.1 Using Staff Feedback Revisit the List of Touch Points One by One

Directions to the event were clear and easy to follow	3/100 (an error occurs three times in 100)
On arrival, there was parking available close to the main building	6/100
Access to the venue was clear with minimal traffic	1/100
The external look of the venue was well maintained and clean	20/100
The lobby had a pleasing ambience and was clean and tidy	8/100
There was no queue at security	16/100
The staff smiled and gave their immediate and undivided attention	4/100
The staff spoke in a clear and calm manner	4/100

each time a problem occurs, so the staff will be able to say how many times out of 100 this particular error occurs. This is why customer feedback, staff feedback, and logging complaints is important (Table 1.1).

Some errors will require a subjective view as it will be difficult for staff to admit that customers are not greeted with a smile, say, and yet many customers experience this.

Some hotels use mystery shoppers to assist with this measurement of management observations. This gives more of a genuine and realistic customer viewpoint by providing a snapshot of touch points at a certain time or a range of times.

To be effective, it is important to get staff buy-in and cooperation, so the exercise should be undertaken in a non-confrontational way with effective communication and an explanation of why the exercise is taking place and its value in achieving total quality. All staff must feel comfortable to admit where service errors occur.

Looking at the above example, it is easy to identify the touch points which are creating the most errors. If this exercise is carried out for the entire customer journey, it can be seen where the faults lie in terms of departmental activities: that is, housekeeping, food and beverage, conference and banqueting points, some of which are shown in Figure 1.7 by way of example.

Viewing the customer journey in this manner can seem daunting at first and may feel like an insurmountable cause to attempt to unpick and improve hundreds of faults that are happening all the time.

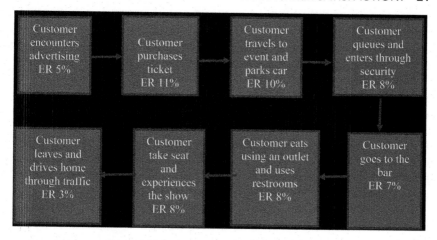

Figure 1.7 Error Rate of Touch Points

INDUSTRY VOICE

"Some of the staff suggestions to reduce errors in the hotel were ingenious, some were clever, but most were completely obvious.

The kind of thing that is so easy to see once you have taken a step back and looked at the problem for either the first time or from a different angle.

These ranged from stock management, simplified processes, new products/concepts and demand management".

Adam Rowledge, Managing Director, Rowledge Associates

To attempt to tackle all the fault areas at once may be a futile exercise and be demoralising. So, a structured step-by-step approach over a longer term should be taken – department by department, perhaps.

By the completion of the error-finding exercise with staff, it is essential to come away with actions and a vision of what the service could look like if the faults were reduced or eliminated. This cannot be a tick-box exercise undertaken without outcomes, so a report of each error should include an action, and it will not be removed from the list of errors until action has corrected the fault. This will require monitoring, so periodic repeats of the error-finding exercise must be undertaken to ensure that the action did fix the error and it is not reoccurring.

Some Managers 'RAG' rate (Red, Amber, Green) the faults not necessarily in order of their frequency but in order of their impact on customer experience.

Other Managers will try to reduce the error rate by tackling the most frequent first.

Whichever priority method is decided, the next step in the process is to select the target and brainstorm ways to improve that area.

In the Lotus example previously used, employees identified over 1,000 ways to improve the car, and the resulting sense of combined effort and teamwork was palpable. Empowered employees will often find solutions which The Manager may never think of by themselves. So, it is wise to use this resource.

There may be cost implications to implementing solutions, and this may result in ideas being rejected, but providing a clear reason will still maintain the process and uphold staff morale.

Once the process of making systematic operational changes is done – made easier by the inherent buy-in from staff – the next stage is to measure the impact of the changes. Use the same measurement criteria as before – whether it was staff feedback, guest complaint percentage, or mystery shopper techniques – and compare the results.

Some of the ideas will have an impact and some may not. Some may even have made things worse. It is therefore important to remeasure the error rates at a predetermined future date. Fault-finding is a continuous review process and needs

INDUSTRY VOICE

"It is important to challenge the status quo constantly. We used to have a pianist playing in the lounge area of the hotel on Friday and Saturday evenings and at Sunday lunch and Afternoon Tea.

Often, they were playing to themselves as guests were either in the bar or in one of the restaurants enjoying dinner.

When I analysed the figures, it was costing in excess of £25,000 per year so I duly cancelled the pianist, sold the piano and installed a music system which provided music to more areas at a fraction of the cost whilst enhancing the guest experience".

David Connell, General Manager, South Lodge 5star Hotel

to be revisited periodically in order to pull ahead of competitors and become known as the event or hotel that gets things right first time and every time.

It will be reassuring for The Manager and the staff to see the error rate fall over time, and hopefully, the amount of time, money, and energy dealing with errors will reduce.

1.3 Total Quality Management

Total Quality Management (TQM) is a concept where quality must not fall below the optimum level because if it does, it cannot be considered TQM.

To facilitate optimum standards at all times to all customers requires pre-empting any potential failure in providing the optimum quality of service to every customer. Mainly, this is done by checking. The Manager must walk around the venue or hotel and check everything is at optimum quality – often, this is delegated to departmental managers, or the head housekeeper, or the assistant events manager.

In hotels, it used to be important for customers to see The Manager visiting all areas of the hotel by walking through each department. It is a social aspect of the role, and customers feel special to be asked by The Manager if everything is to their satisfaction. It is how The Manager gets to know the customers. There is deeper purpose to this activity, however. By walking through the hotel, The Manager is performing a checking exercise to determine optimum quality and service is being achieved and pre-empt any issues before they impact the customer. It is TQM to ask a diner in the restaurant if everything is to their satisfaction and deal with it at that point of contact than to fail that customer's expectations and pick it up when they challenge the bill or complain to reception as they leave the hotel. This is called Service Recovery which can be recovered during the point where the customer is consuming the service (in the restaurant) but cannot be recovered after the service has consumed (at reception).

It is no less important at events. The Manager has opportunities to visit all areas of the venue to check everything is progressing according to what has been planned. This means visiting the kitchen to check with the chef, visiting the production box to check with the production manager, and walking through the event space to check the set-up, decoration, branding, etc.

A reporting structure needs to be in place so that any faults which might impact the customer experience and threaten TQM get reported quickly to the relevant person so they can be prioritised and corrected. It could be a broken light bulb, a squeaking door, or a blocked drain. This is what hotel room attendants report and head housekeepers check for. Event managers should do the same by walking through the venue regularly and certainly before the doors open for customers to enter the event.

AUTHOR'S VOICE

When I teach events management, I segment the job of the events manager into three distinct sections: pre-event, during-event, and post-event.

Pre-event is where all the planning happens during the lead-in (the time between an event is confirmed as going ahead and the actual date of an event happening). I allocate 95% of the event manager's job to the pre-event planning stage.

During-event is where all the checking happens onsite on the day of an event. Checking everything that was planned is now happening. I allocate 3% of the event manager's job to the 'checking' stage.

Post-event is where the after-event procedures happen such as paying final bills, conducting the debriefs, and conducting the evaluation and feedback. I allocate the final 2% to the post-event stage.

Although the actual percentages are not necessarily accurate and will vary from event to event, this method does highlight two important aspects. First, it can be seen that the post-event procedures make up 2% of the 100% job of the event manager which means that if The Manager does not perform the debriefs, evaluation, and feedback, they are not doing the total of their job (many event managers do not bother with post-event procedures because they do not understand the value of doing so).

Second, it is surprising to students that I consider the onsite part of the job on the day of an event to be a little as 3% of the job when they might have thought it was the busiest part of event management. This directs their consideration to the value and complexity of planning an event and also to the understanding that the job for an events manager on the day of an event is to check, check, and check.

I say that the event manager's job is not to 'do' the event, but to 'run' the event which can only be achieved by standing back and overseeing (checking) that what has been planned is now happening. This is essential for the event to run smoothly, safely, and to meet its objectives.

AUTHOR'S VOICE

I always conduct a 'final walk-round' of the venue for each event I organise. I will not open the doors without undertaking this procedure.

If I run out of time and the doors are due to open, I will not allow the venue to open until my final walk-round is complete.

It can mean a delay in opening the doors. Venue managers hate this. Clients don't like it, either. I once had a sponsor shouting at me in a frenzy because I refused to open the doors on time.

But safety is my priority which is not the same priority a sponsor may have. It is most important that I have checked for safety before customers enter the space.

In my experience, I have found it a positive aspect to open the doors late. Customers gather outside and the excitement builds so that when the doors do open ten minutes or so late, there is a rush of customers into the venue and the event is in full flow from the outset. This is far better than opening the doors on time and having one or two early customers wander into an empty venue with no atmosphere.

The worst thing, for me, is when the doors open without anyone knowing about it and suddenly there are customers in the venue and the staff are not ready for them. That is why I always open the doors late.

Depending on the impact of the fault on the customer experience (remembering that every impact is important in maintaining TQM), it may be necessary to have a preventative maintenance schedule. This is where equipment is checked and maintained periodically before it could fail because it is a piece of equipment that is essential to the smooth running of the business or it would have significant detrimental impact on the customer experience if it fails.

Light bulbs do not require preventative maintenance because if a light bulb fails it can be replaced quickly and cheaply and will not have a significant detrimental impact on the smooth running of the business or the customer experience (as long as there is a reporting procedure to ensure the light bulb is replaced quickly to ensure TQM).

Whereas if an air-conditioning unit fails, it can take time for an engineer to attend, and whilst it is faulty, it is impacting the customer experience and failing TQM. It is essential therefore to have a preventative maintenance plan for air-conditioning so that it receives scheduled maintenance and a fault would be identified before the unit fails.

Preventative maintenance is what we all do with our cars. We have our car serviced to prevent it breaking down and giving us a problem. This is far better than waiting for it to fail and then having to deal with the problem in the rain on the side of a busy road.

Preventative maintenance can be scheduled, whereas if a fault occurs, it will require urgent fixing at the time it goes wrong which could be during the middle of service or during a wedding. Scheduled maintenance can be planned for convenience – if it is the air-conditioning, for example, it would be scheduled for maintenance in the winter or when the business is not busy.

Although there is an unnecessary cost with planned preventative maintenance because The Manager is paying for an engineer to service the equipment when it does not need it, it can work out cheaper than having to repair an item which has damaged because it was not maintained or the fault was not spotted in time.

It also might cost more for urgent callout fees and repairs than a preventative maintenance plan. Engineers charge premiums when they know it is a piece of equipment that is vital for the running of your business.

So, in maintaining TQM, it must be determined what is the impact on customer service and the smooth running of the business, and what are the financial implications between a preventative maintenance schedule versus repairs to an item which has failed.

Then, the business should have a maintenance schedule for each piece of equipment in the business to show whether the asset is on a preventative maintenance plan, what is the periodic maintenance cycle such as monthly or twice-yearly, who is the company contracted to perform the service, and what is the manufacturer's or the legal requirement for maintaining that item of equipment.

In the case of a fire alarm system, there are legal requirements for preventative maintenance and checking so that it does not fail when it is needed. Such is the impact on the running of the business and threat to customers and staff if the alarm should fail and a fire goes undetected.

AUTHOR'S VOICE

A perfect example of TQM is a hot buffet where the first customer to arrive at the buffet is greeted with full trays of piping hot food.

The twentieth customer at the buffet must also receive the same standard of quality, as should the last customer who arrives late. This is TQM.

It means that the venue must have procedures in place to ensure that the buffet is constantly replenished. This can be done by not putting all dishes onto the buffet at the beginning of service but holding back some for replenishing as well as transferring half-empty trays onto smaller ones so that they look full.

Because of this need to uphold TQM for each customer who visits the buffet, I never place a buffet table against a wall. I always allow enough room from the wall for a member of service staff to get behind and keep the buffet stocked and replenished. It is essential if every customer is to receive the same service whenever they attend the buffet.

Providing staff with access behind the buffet is also a courtesy for good service because a member of staff can answer questions from customers such as ingredients and allergens. And if the buffet becomes busy, that staff member can assist with service onto plates to speed the flow and monitor portion control.

It is surprising how many venues put out a buffet and think the job is done, then leave it unattended.

1.4 Service Quality Management (SERVQUAL)

The SERVQUAL model (shown in Figure 1.8) is considered to be important for defining customer satisfaction. It makes use of a technique called 'gap analysis' to demonstrate how The Manager can improve the quality level of customer service. These 'gaps' are:

1   The gap between consumers' expectations and management's perceptions of consumers' expectations

2   The gap between management's perceptions of consumers' expectations and service quality specifications

3   The gap between service quality specifications and service delivery

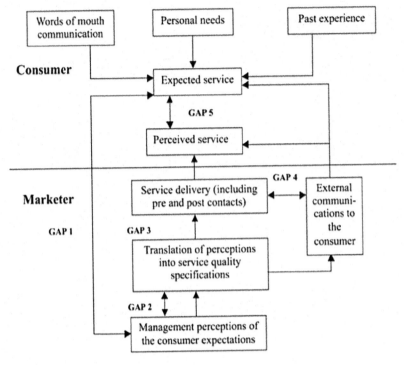

Source: Parasuraman *et al.* (1985)

Figure 1.8 SERVQUAL Model
Source: Parasuraman et al. (1985)

4   The gap between service delivery and external communications to consumers

5   The gap between consumers' expectations and perceived service

(Augustyn and Ho, 1998, pp.74–75)

1.5 Customer Balanced Scorecard

The Balanced Scorecard (shown in Figure 1.9) is a model developed by Kaplan and Norton (1996) to depict the need to measure a range of factors of performance beyond only financial and profit performance. It was designed to lead businesses from the conventional focus on financial performance as the measure of their success. Contemporary thinking now expects businesses to consider other success factors, as the model depicts. There are four perspectives which are considered to provide the balanced score of success. These are: Customer Perspective; Learning/Growth Perspective; Internal Process Perspective; and Financial Perspective.

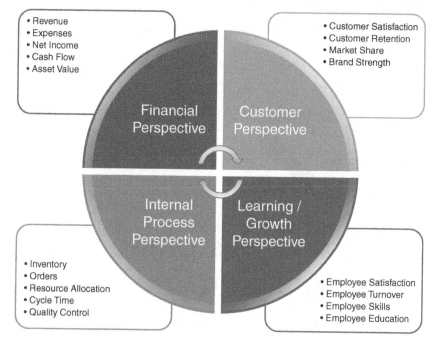

Figure 1.9 Balanced Scorecard
Source: bi-insider.com

Within the perspective of customers is customer satisfaction, customer retention, market share, and brand strength.

By looking at the four perspectives of the Balanced Scorecard and measuring our performance against the criteria within each perspective, it can be seen that The Manager will regard customers as highly as learning and growth, internal processes, and finances. Focusing on all four perspectives is a balanced viewpoint of performance rather than leading with finance or considering only finance.

References

Augustyn, M., and Ho, S.K. (1998) 'Service Quality and Tourism', *Journal of Travel Research*, 37(1). doi: 10.1177/004728759803700110.

Kaplan, R.S., and Norton, D.P. (1996) *The Balanced Scorecard*. Cambridge, MA: Harvard College.

Parasuraman, A., Zeithaml, V.A., and Berry, L.L. (1988) 'SERVQUAL: A Multiple-Item Scale for Measuring Consumer Perceptions of Service Quality', *Journal of Retailing*, 64(1), pp. 12–40.

Chapter **2**

Why Is Customer Satisfaction Important?

This chapter begins with recognising why customers become returning customers and how important it is to convert new customers to becoming return customers. We ask how The Manager knows they are not satisfying their customers which leads to the learning value of conducting structured feedback. We look at why evaluation needs to be embedded into the procedures at events and hotels, and how evaluation should be conducted. We offer eight suggestions of how to generate customer feedback.

Section 2.0 visits the value of reputation and professionalism in regulating what is an unregulated industry. Here, we look at the use of external resources and the value of maintaining a list of approved suppliers.

Section 2.1 looks at the costs of not achieving customer satisfaction.

Every Manager wants their customers to be satisfied and happy. If they did not want this, they would not be managing an event or a hotel.

For one thing, an event or hotel would not make money in the long term to sustain the future of the business if its customers were dissatisfied, demanded refunds, did not want to return in the future, or spread negative information.

DOI: 10.4324/9781003154600-3

Without money coming into the business from customers, there is no business. No event or hotel can survive without generating revenue.

So, although having happy customers provides The Manager with a good feeling and demonstrates a job well done, it is really about making money.

There is nothing wrong in The Manager recognising and accepting they want their customers to be happy so that more money is achieved from them. It is not greed; it is good business.

Once this point is accepted, it can be understood that customers bring money to the business.

The more customers, the more money. Better still – we want more customers to return and continue returning to spend their money. This is why customer satisfaction is important.

Why it is better to have more customers returning and keep returning is because it is easier and cheaper to have customers returning to an event or hotel they have visited before.

New customers need to find out about an event or hotel and that can only be achieved through advertising and promotion which reaches them. Advertising costs money. Whereas a customer who has visited before and is happy to return costs the business nothing because the customer is already aware.

The key is in linking the two – making new customers become returning customers.

Once a new customer experiences the event or hotel for the first time – those touch points, again – The Manager needs to ensure that they will return. And they will return only if they received good customer service which met their expectations.

If new customers are happy with the customer experience they receive, they will return and keep returning.

There is just one chance to win a customer and ensure they return. It has to happen the first time they visit, at that initial point of contact. If that first time of attending an event or visiting a hotel is not successful, the customer is lost and will likely not return.

It is very difficult to recover a customer once they have left an event or hotel which did not meet their expectations. Okay, they might give it a second chance

AUTHOR'S VOICE

I worked at a multipurpose venue where all inbound phone enquiries were received by the receptionist. But sometimes the receptionist could be busy with other duties and responsibilities in that hectic front-office environment – anything from answering phones, to photocopying, to making coffee for visitors. These diversions meant that the receptionist may not answer the phone before the prospective customer hangs up. It is impossible to know how many times that happened or what the enquiry would have been and how much revenue it could have brought into the business.

Also, the receptionist was not an experienced event organiser. So, if an enquiry for an event was received at reception, the receptionist might not deal with it in the correct manner. This might be because they are not familiar with event terminology and the customer enquiring might judge this to be an unprofessional venue and not suitable to host their prestigious event.

Or it could be that the customer asks a question such as, "How many people can your banqueting suite hold?" and the receptionist may answer, "200". The customer might then say, "Oh, that's a pity because I have 230 guests. Never mind, thanks anyway. Goodbye". Here, the customer's business is lost because the receptionist did not know to ask whether it was a sit-down or standing event, and is it a banquet or a buffet, and is it on round tables or theatre style. Perhaps, the food could be served in the restaurant in order to accommodate 230 guests in the banqueting suite. Anyway, an experienced event manager knows that it is usual for actual numbers to drop because a customer with an enquiry will always seek capacity for the maximum number of guests and they usually over-anticipate how many guests there will be.

When I went to the conference and banqueting office at this venue and asked how many event customers made an enquiry to reception in the last month, they did not know. When I asked how many customers were lost last month, they did not know. When I asked the ratio of enquiries to losses – how many enquiries converted to confirmed bookings – they did not know. And when I asked the reason customers did not convert to confirmed bookings, they did not know. That is a lot of unknowns.

I installed a direct phone line to the conference and banqueting office so enquiries were dealt with by event staff who had the experience and confidence to answer questions in a professional manner and discuss options with potential customers. This provided better customer service from the outset of the enquiry stage and could build immediate rapport with a potential customer to achieve the sale.

This also provided data for how many enquiries were being received at any period, where were the peaks and troughs of enquiries so that promotion campaigns could be planned in the troughs, where the enquiries were coming from so it could be seen how effective advertising is, and we could measure the conversion rate from enquiries to confirmed bookings as well as identify reasons enquiries were not converting.

Another important factor arising from this change was retaining the details of customers whose enquiry did not convert to a confirmed booking. They are still potential customers for other events or smaller events. Their numbers might reduce, or if this venue was not available but now we have a cancellation, we can follow up the enquiry. All enquiries are targets for future promotion campaigns: for example, if I knew an enquiry was lost because it went to another venue, I would follow up after the event to see if the customer was happy with that venue's services, quality, and costs because if they weren't, I could win that client from a competitor. A busy receptionist turning away business would not record the details of lost customers.

If it is not possible to install a dedicated phone line to the events office, the reception staff should be instructed to take only the contact details of customers who make an enquiry. The receptionist does not need to engage in conversation with them or answer their questions. Just take the contact details and inform the customer that a team member from the events department will be in touch.

Then, the customer's contact details get passed to the events department in a procedural fashion for them to follow up and deal with the enquiry using their knowledge and experience of client management, enquiry handling, and event management.

but The Manager will not know how many customers are not returning to give it a second chance, so the losses are incalculable.

The first point of customer contact – whether it is a customer walking into an event, a guest checking-in to a hotel, or a customer making a telephone enquiry – is the opportunity to get the customer service experience right. From the outset, the customer must experience great customer service.

Often, it is that first point of contact which gets mishandled and the customer sets off on their journey from a dissatisfied standpoint.

It can often be the case that much effort and thought has been given to customer service in certain areas where it is obvious to please customers such as welcome, arrival, foodservice, and bar service. But less consideration is given to that first point of customer contact before they arrive to the event or hotel. The first phone call or email; the enquiry; the questions, information gathering, or need for directions. These first points of contact set the customer's frame of mind and their expectations for the next stage of their journey which *will* be the welcome, the arrival, or going to the bar or restaurant.

Not every Manager knows that they are not satisfying their customers. Deep down they may have an inkling, and if they stopped what they are doing on a day-to-day basis and sat down to think about it, the signs will be there to confirm it to them. So, how do you know if you are not satisfying your customers?

Let's ask this from the other perspective: how do you know if you *are* satisfying your customers?

You ask them.

The Manager needs to introduce processes into the business which asks customers whether they are pleased with the service they experienced as a customer.

Here, The Manager needs to think about what answers they want to know so that they know which questions to ask the customer. If The Manager wants to know how the customer experienced the welcome at the front door, they ask the question: 'Did you receive a friendly and polite welcome when you arrived?'

It is not enough simply to ask these questions. Sure, it is polite and courteous to ask customers if they had a good time or enjoyed their stay, but this is informal, unstructured feedback, and is unreliable.

The Manager cannot rely on what customers say because people tend not to be honest in face-to-face situations. Customers may feel embarrassed or intimidated, or they may feel it is not worth complaining about – especially if it is a minor issue not worth fussing over. Also, it would not be worth making a complaint if the customer is unlikely to return – a one-off event or hotel stay, or because they live abroad, perhaps. Besides these, the usual way of asking customers is by closed questions, to say, 'Did you enjoy your time with us?' and the likely response to that would be for the customer to say, 'Yes, thank you'.

It does not tell us what we want to know about their experience whilst they were with us. It is not structured or in-depth, and it is not tailored to areas of our business we need to learn about – customers do not know what goes into running an event or a hotel, so asking them without structured questions about what we want to learn, is not going to help us.

Another problem with informal feedback is that customers may be influenced by other people, or at an event they may be under the influence of alcohol and are so merry that they will tell you whatever you want to hear, including that they love you! Or they might just want to get home and not want to be delayed by a discussion about their experiences.

It is not convenient to stand at the front doors of a venue or hotel and ask every guest what they thought of their experience and what areas of our business we might improve – there is no time for that type of approach, and it would be inappropriate. We are never going to achieve any depth of feedback that way.

But, as mentioned above, it is a polite and courteous way to thank customers by asking if they enjoyed their time, so it is still worthwhile to do.

By doing this – asking questions at the end of an event or hotel stay – The Manager may get that inkling of things being well or not. But it can now be seen it is only an inkling and that is not enough to achieve 100% customer satisfaction.

To achieve honest, in-depth, balanced, and considered views from customers, The Manager needs to conduct structured feedback and evaluation procedures.

Some managers believe that they do not have time for feedback and evaluation after an event has happened or after a guest has checked out. But if The Manager thinks there is no time for this vital learning activity, it is only because they do not recognise the great value to their business by checking the experience of their customers which can only be achieved by feedback and evaluation.

Feedback and evaluation activities are planned before an event – in the planning stages. It does not take time afterwards to plan it. Nor does it take time to action it – the customer does that. The customer sits down to fill out an evaluation questionnaire. All The Manager has to do is send it, which takes no time at all. No: lack of time is not the reason for failing to conduct feedback and evaluation.

Time does not prevent feedback and evaluation – poor planning does that

Thought needs to be given to who will conduct the feedback – that is, who is going to be sending it out. Will it be the organiser, the client, or the venue. Often, it is more convenient for the client to send the feedback questionnaire to guests because they will have the attendance list and contact details of those who attended – especially if it is a staff event or a conference with delegates. If it is a ticketed concert, it would be the event organiser who has the database of customers who purchased tickets and would therefore send the evaluation questionnaire.

In all cases, it must be determined who did actually attend so that the questionnaire gets sent to actual attendees and not those who confirmed they would attend or bought a ticket but actually did not come (unless the questionnaire is designed to ask why they chose not to attend).

Then, it needs to be thought about what questions will be asked. If the client is sending it out, they will want to know whether their guests enjoyed the event – what they liked and disliked. But the organiser and the venue might want to ask something as well. So, the questionnaire should be constructed with questions from whomever requires feedback. The venue might want to know about the quality of service, the standard of catering, or how easy it was to find the venue, whereas the organiser might want to know whether customers enjoyed the show. This is where identifying the stakeholder groups (see Section 1.2) is valuable because each stakeholder might be invited to insert one or two questions into the feedback questionnaire. A sponsor, for example, might want to know how many guests noticed who sponsored the event or whether they sampled a product during their visit and would they buy it in future. An event caterer might want to ascertain how many customers ate from the buffet, did they feel that the range of food options was sufficient, and was the food of a high quality to meet their expectations.

It needs to be decided to whom the feedback will be sent. Will it be to all actual attendees (total population) or to a selected proportion of them (sample population) such as 25% or perhaps 50 out of 100 attendees. If it is a mass-participant event, it might be better to focus the questionnaire to 20% or 50% which is enough to determine patterns in the responses, such as 90% of those questioned enjoyed the show. Identifying sub-groups of stakeholders (see Section 1.2) can be advantageous to determine responses from family guests, VIPs, or dining guests only, for instance.

Consideration needs to be given to what method will be used. Feedback is usually conducted by an email survey for speed, efficiency, and convenience, but there are other methods such as focus groups and debrief meetings. The method chosen could affect how many responses are achieved – it is easy and time-efficient to complete an email questionnaire but not many people might make the time and effort to attend a post-event debriefing session. As a general rule, an email questionnaire should be around ten questions and take no longer than ten minutes to complete. Any more arduous and people might not bother to start it or will abandon it partway through completion. For this reason, it is a good idea to include information about the reason for the questionnaire, how many questions there are and how short it will take to complete.

Incentives can be used to entice customers to complete a survey, such as entering a prize draw for future tickets to an event or afternoon tea for two in a hotel. This is a valuable technique to secure post-event or post-stay customer engagement and obtain customer data for future marketing activities.

At periodic times of year, focus groups and debrief meetings will help provide constructive feedback from former customers. With former customers, an incentive may be offered to encourage their participation in the survey. It is a good way to continue engagement and relationships with former customers or reward them with a discount or visit in return for their participation so it generates ongoing return business. For venues and hotels with corporate clientele, August can be a quiet period so it can be a good idea to engage with former customers who might want to participate with a survey and be encouraged to visit at that time when business is low. August is also a good time for corporate clients to plan for Christmas, so a well-timed survey could inspire them to forward-plan their event or booking with you.

It can be seen how important it is for feedback activities to be planned in advance – certainly pre-event. It is not viable to consider the questions and methods of evaluation after an event has finished. It will be too late and people will have moved on. If it is not planned, it will not happen.

The survey has to be conducted immediately following the event. This is where time is important, not the fact that there is no time for it. As already identified, feedback and evaluation is about planning, not lack of time.

Hotels are more stable than events. Hotels have longevity. So it requires the feedback and evaluation procedures to be planned just once so they can be conducted each time a guest has checked out. Once feedback and evaluation has been undertaken it can be repeated, although the questions and methods will need monitoring and adjusting from time to time.

Events do not have that luxury – the questions and methods will need consideration from event to event, venue to venue, and client to client but may not need to be changed.

What is key to hotels and events is ensuring that the feedback and evaluation is a *procedure* which means that it becomes embedded in the standard operating practices and never gets left out. Consistency of quality, standards, and meeting customer service expectations is essential, so it cannot happen that a procedure gets overlooked or is conducted ad hoc – that would make it an activity, not a procedure.

Procedures must be followed, so the excuses of 'not enough time', or 'this is a routine event so it doesn't need evaluation', or 'this is a small event', or 'this guest has stayed with us before' do not become the get-outs that prevent monitoring of standards and learning from our customers' experience of our service.

It is only partially helpful to achieve feedback from some areas of the customer experience but not others or in some areas of the business and not in others.

It is a mistake for a venue or hotel to conduct feedback and evaluation for weddings but not conferences or at events with 100 or more guests but not at events with under 100 guests. Some hotels make the mistake of evaluating big or unusual events but not their routine events such as wakes or small meetings. If a customer is dissatisfied at any type of event of any size, it needs to be identified and corrected.

If it is a procedure, it must happen at every event and for every customer to ensure consistency with providing the customer service experience.

No manager can claim 100% customer satisfaction if only 60% of customers are asked

Quality is consistency

Some managers conduct feedback for large events but not smaller ones; or for weddings but not conferences; or for VIP customers but not for other customers. This is never the right way to conduct procedures. Procedures must be consistent for every customer. It must be consistent. Consistency is what makes a procedure, a procedure.

Procedures must be consistent to ensure customer service is consistent

Here are some suggestions of how to generate customer feedback:

1   **Post a link or Quick Response (QR) code to a survey on social media**

    Either as part of another post or a post on its own, this method can generate feedback. Beware that social media users have low levels of attention and patience, so the survey needs to be shorter if using this method.

2   **Offer a prize**

    Offering something for free will get people's attention. One option is to have followers complete a survey to enter the contest. Or send the survey after they have entered the contest.

3   **Create a live process for obtaining feedback from customers**

    Customers might think of ways your site could be better when they are using it, but they might not have time to provide verbal feedback. Put in place a mechanism to report faults.

4   Stay on top of social media channels

Direct-message (DM) customers and respond to comments to see how people feel about your event or hotel. Quick response times are expected. Using technology, some companies can do this as the event goes wrong, in real time for instance. This tracks trends and fixes problems in front of future customers as they happen.

5   Request feedback on the booking confirmation

It is important to manage the booking process as well as the quality at the time of arrival. Sometimes these can be months apart. Have a separate survey to cover this and ask about improvements to the site or dealings with the sales team, and if any difficulties were encountered during the booking process.

6   Create an online community

Facebook and Instagram groups and hashtags can start online groups which are prime for gathering insight. It does require continuous monitoring and a moderator, but the engagement strengthens your relationship with customers as well as generating feedback and ideas.

7   Request feedback when a booking is lost

Knowing why someone did not become a customer is valuable feedback. Sometimes it is more valuable than feedback from actual customers. Is it something that can be fixed and gain market share? Is it a glaring fault for a small segment, such as disabled access, for instance? To make it easier to get a response from the departing customer, create a multiple-choice list to share the reason (or reasons) for cart abandonment.

8   Send out email surveys to new customers

New customers are keen to engage, so take the initiative and gain some market intelligence about booking systems as well as their expectations.

It does take education to know what is going wrong. And it takes education to know how to reflect, analyse, and interpret what is wrong. It takes education to know how to implement change to make things right. It takes education to know to measure performance and to know how to set Key Performance Indicators (KPIs) to measure performance against.

But it does not take education only. After all, not every event or hotel manager who holds a relevant qualification is good at their job or has all the knowledge required to achieve 100% customer satisfaction. It also takes experience. Experience teaches what is wrong and how to make it right, to not continue to repeat it.

Learning comes from education and from experience, so The Manager can merge the two from the feedback of each customer and start to learn from their experience.

Once gathered, feedback needs to be shared. The Manager needs to be brave about that. The point of conducting feedback and evaluation is to receive open and honest responses from all customers. It cannot stop there. It must follow through to being open and honest with those who are providing the service to customers.

Solutions need to be identified in response to what customers are saying. Actions need to be taken. It is fruitless to go through the exercise of obtaining feedback if half the staff are unaware what the customers are reporting of the experience they received.

Feedback and evaluation is for learning. It teaches how customers are experiencing the service they receive; it teaches what is right; it teaches what needs improving; and it has to teach staff where they are succeeding and failing when providing service to their customers.

The learning then becomes action points. If no actions are taken to correct or improve the customer service experience, it will not develop the staff and improve their performance. Errors will get repeated. More customers will experience the same shortfalls and disappointments. We have to learn.

It would be a failure of management if a second customer experiences a shortfall in our service which a first customer has already experienced.

AUTHOR'S VOICE

In my experience, staff are delighted to learn how they are performing. They relish knowing when they have been recognised for doing their job to the customers' satisfaction.

Okay, staff may not relish being informed where they are failing, but I find staff are willing and happy to be shown how they can develop their customer service skills such as communication, procedures, and problem solving.

All staff want to develop either in their career progression or in their knowledge and skills even if they are comfortable to stay in the job and level where they are. They all want to do their job well.

It serves no purpose to withhold customer feedback just because it is embarrassing, disappointing, or highlights our failures.

Events management and hotel management are unregulated industries in terms of requiring professional qualifications to be able to do the job. It does not even require a minimum experience, apprenticeship, or training. A doctor must be qualified, as must an optician, a pharmacist, and a school teacher. But anyone can put on an event or run a hotel without regulated qualifications to do so.

This is why there are many bad events and poorly run hotels: because the industry is awash with unqualified and inexperienced event organisers and hotel managers. It is not necessarily a bad thing. It means that there are low barriers to entry and many opportunities to enter events and hotel management. It also means that there is greater chance of standing out for getting it absolutely right!

Many people find themselves in events management and hotel management roles by accident, and they can do the job very well by gaining practical experience and know-how. But, how do they know they are doing it right if they have not been formally taught and educated in the specialisms? That is down to customers telling them they are doing a good job: feedback and evaluation.

What regulates the industry is professionalism. Professionalism differentiates good event and hotel managers from the not-so-good managers. This makes it easy to be an event or hotel manager and easy to be a good one. It does not require certificates to shine in the job; it requires polished professionalism gained from learning from experience.

Experience + Learning = Professionalism (E + L = P)

This is not to say that formal qualifications are not available in the professions of catering, events management, hotel management, tourism management, and leisure management. Experience takes much time to acquire, but degree qualifications provide specialist competencies and understandings in shorter time frames so that graduates can enter the industry with knowledge and basic skills as the foundation for their continued experience and learning.

The events and hotel industries are made up of a mixture of qualified and unqualified managers which is why there is wide variation in the standards and quality of customer service and a few dissatisfied customers. There are managers who do not know what they are doing wrong or that they are doing anything wrong at all.

But, getting it right is the reward. It is important to get it right. And it is important to get it right from the outset of the customer's journey.

AUTHOR'S VOICE

The Edge Hotel School at the University of Essex is the first hotel school in the UK and the only university with a fully commercial 4* country house hotel on its campus.

Students study for a degree in events management or hotel management with the traditional theoretical components of lectures, seminars, and assessments to provide them with academic knowledge and understanding in areas such as finance, managing people, leadership, creative event production, and customer service. When students enter industry, they carry these competencies with them into their roles.

Whereas most universities send their students out for a year to work in industry to gain practical skills, Edge students gain their practical experience during their academic study and lectures by working in the hotel on campus. In their first year, they are operational staff; in the second year, they become supervisory staff by supervising the first-year students; and in the third year, they perform managerial roles such as duty management and night management.

By working across all departments of the hotel in a structured study and assessment environment, Edge students graduate with both theoretical management knowledge and practical skills and competences – what they call 'industry ready'. This helps the industry evolve with professionals at entry level who have knowledge, understanding, skills, and confidence to lead their inexperienced or unqualified staff to perform professionally and provide excellent customer service.

There are no minimum standards in the events and hotel industry. But the industry does regulate itself through awards and accreditations which inform customers into the standards and quality of events and hotels, the most widely recognised being the AA star and rosette ratings but there are many others.

Awards and accreditations help teach managers to do things the right way, and it motivates management and staff to continue to strive to deliver higher quality and service so they achieve or retain their industry recognition in the form of awards and accreditations.

On the downside, there are no guarantees in an unregulated industry – the customer does not know that the event they are attending is organised by an educated, trained, or experienced professional. Neither would a customer know if the hotel they are staying in is run by an educated, trained, or experienced hotelier (unless there is accreditation to notify them).

This introduces risk. There is risk in harm and safety if The Manager is not educated in current safety regulations and practices. Safety aside, there are risks throughout all the touch points during the customer journey such as food hygiene and customer service.

To some extent, customers do not care. They are not interested in the structure of the events and hotel industry and are not aware of the risks. That is somebody else's job to worry about – it is *your* job. Customers just want a good experience at an event and a good stay at a hotel. So long as it does not go wrong, they will leave happy and naïve. And it is the job of The Manager to make this so.

2.0 The Value of Reputation

The reputation of an event or a hotel is crucial for long-term sustainability of the business. It is the job of The Manager to protect the reputation of their event or hotel.

Whereas an event manager might think this is less important for them because the event will come around and then it will be gone, there are two elements with events which rely on the value of good reputation.

The first is the legacy of an event. Yes, the event might be gone but its legacy will live on. People remember things – especially problematic things. Even when an event legacy fades it could make a resurgence. Supposing that event comes around again, or takes place in a different location, or it was not supposed to happen again but there is demand or a request to do it again. This is where its legacy resurfaces. In the era of social media, it is easy to rekindle a legacy or do a quick online search to reveal the history of an event including the comments, reviews, and Likes. Search for *Fyre Festival* and you will get the idea.

The second reason why reputation matters for events is the professional reputation of The Manager. If an event has not delivered to the expectations of customers and there is negative PR, it will reflect poorly on the person who organised that event. The events industry is a 'community of practice' (Brown and Stokes, 2021), whereby a socio-professional structure networks people who work in the same field. Not only clients who talk to other clients but also venues, caterers, decorators, technicians, other event organisers, and all other suppliers to events – they all talk to each other and swap good ideas and horror stories. It is this social construct which connects the industry, so it will never stop.

It is therefore impossible to maintain a good reputation as an event organiser and gain new jobs by referral if customers are unhappy with your events.

I have organised events for blue-chip corporations, celebrities, international music stars, and royalty. But I have never won a job by advertising my services.

I have only ever won clients by networking, word of mouth, and reputation. I only keep clients by delivering 100% customer service.

For three consecutive years, I provided all backstage hospitality at The BRIT Awards but I wasn't selected from an advert. And I was invited back in years two and three because of my reputation from the previous years which meant I could be relied upon to provide excellent customer service to VIPs, celebrities, and artists who attend backstage at the BRITs.

Every Manager must consider the reputation of their event, hotel, or venue. Let's not forget it is personal as well as professional reputation at stake.

If it is a repeat event such as an annual music festival, the impacts of a damaged reputation are more significant and can impact ticket sales and attendance at the next festival.

"Your reputation is all you have and therefore needs to be guarded well. Good reputations are hard to build and easy to lose.

During the COVID-19 pandemic we decided to be as flexible as possible and allow clients to move and rebook events with no penalty. Where possible we kept this flexible approach right the way through the year – transferring deposits, shifting dates again and again, and very rarely charging cancellation fees.

This gained us the reputation of a fair business partner and actually brought us new business as conference agents and clients that we had dealt with brought other pieces of business to us because they appreciated our integrity and flexibility. They trusted us, and our reputation as a fair event hotel, that our clients want to work with, has grown and grown and has been well worth the effort".

Sally Beck, General Manager, Royal Lancaster Hotel, London

It is known that it takes a very long time to build a good reputation but a very short time for reputation to be damaged. Recovery from a damaged reputation is long and difficult. The business will suffer during the recovery period, and profits will be impacted because of negative word of mouth. This is why a good reputation must be protected.

For venues and hotels, reputation is everything because word travels about good venues and hotels. But word travels wider and faster if a venue or hotel develops a poor reputation. It can take a great amount of hard work to develop a good reputation, and maintain it, but it is extremely easy to lose it.

Remember, it is not only customers who rely on what other people say about the reputation of a venue or hotel, it is also the people networking within the industry – suppliers, contractors, technical suppliers, florists, decorators, caterers, etc.

Do not forget, also, that the staff who move around within the industry carry their stories with them. It is always worthwhile to release staff on good terms because they may wish to return but also they will go on to work with other industry people and transport your reputation with them.

Exit interviews are valuable to learn from staff why they are choosing to leave your business. It allows open and honest discussion because, finally, the staff member has nothing to lose or fear, now they are leaving you. But if managed delicately, exit interviews provide the feedback from that stakeholder group – the staff – about you as a manager and the business you are running. We should want to find out how we are doing as a manager, leader, or employer.

At the end of the exit interview, there should be an opportunity to part on good terms – even to apologise if there was a failure somewhere such as with communication or workload. The objective here is for the leaving member of staff to feel better about your business when they move to their next position because they will certainly be measuring and benchmarking their experiences from one employer to another. Would it not be helpful if they introduced to their new job the good practices from your managerial style and procedures, rather than tell their new employer how unhappy they were working with you?

So, have you ever asked yourself how a member of staff who left you is going to be talking about you?

If staff are let go, The Manager should remember that each member of staff was at the beginning interviewed and offered the job. They went through your recruitment procedures and were invited to accept the job. If it did not work out, that is a shame. But what is it about the employer/employee relationship that failed? If your recruitment and employment procedures allowed that person into the business, which side failed the other?

AUTHOR'S VOICE

I do not like my customers arranging their own suppliers. Weddings are the difficult ones. There can be the bride or bride's mother who knows a cakemaker. The groom's father knows a disc jockey. But I don't have a relationship with that cakemaker or that DJ so I cannot fully rely on them or trust they will deliver what was promised. I cannot trust that these friend-suppliers will behave in a professional manner.

Supposing the cake looks awful, or collapses, it gets delivered late or doesn't arrive at all? What if the DJ plays music which doesn't fit the profile of the guests or he gets drunk? These are risks that I do not like to take because they are not within my control.

The problem is that if anything goes wrong, it reflects both on me as the organiser and the venue but not the cakemaker or the DJ.

I once organised a VIP launch event in a foreign country and the client insisted on a London club DJ being flown out to entertain the guests. Well, he missed the flight, arrived late, and when he eventually got on the decks, the crowd hated his music! Some guests asked me to pull him off the decks or get him to change his playlist, but I hadn't contracted him, so I had no say over him.

This wasn't the client's fault because they weren't aware of the risks and what could go wrong. To them, it was simply a good idea. It was my fault for relinquishing control.

The answer is to use approved suppliers only – those which have proved their trustfulness or are well-known to have a good reputation. Trust in one's suppliers is everything when protecting your reputation.

If a customer insists that their auntie Anita will supply the wedding cake and their brother Brian will spin the discs, The Manager should arrange a meeting with them to agree the terms such as early delivery of the cake and what is the music playlist. DJ Brian could be given a trial run and Anita might provide a sample cake.

Draw up a contract (see Chapter 5, *Contracts*) setting out what has been agreed and to set the expectations – this will encourage Anita and Brian to adopt a professional approach and treat their role as a contractual agreement rather than just a favour for a relative.

Whereas an event can come and go, venues and hotels have longevity, so their good reputation is essential for the sustainability of the business. To protect their reputation, venues must never relinquish control to other parties such as clients, event organisers, suppliers, or caterers. It is essential to control every element and aspect of what is happening within the venue to ensure the reputation is protected.

If something goes wrong or service is poor, customers will naturally believe it is the venue at fault because it takes place in the venue and always reflects on the venue. For example, if an outside caterer is brought into the venue to provide food for a wedding, and the food is not good, customers will blame the venue. They will not stop to consider whether the food was provided by an outside caterer or not, or who that caterer was, they will only think as far as the venue they are in whilst experiencing food that is not good.

Even if customers are aware the food is provided by an outside caterer and not the venue – if The Manager tells them because complaints have been received, for instance – it still will not matter because customers will forevermore tell the story of the time they experienced poor food at that venue. And The Manager cannot control what people go on to say once they have left the venue. It will be too late.

The Manager at a venue must take steps to ensure that the service quality is maintained at all times by all staff and suppliers. After all, it is not the fault of the customer if the service quality they experience is not up to the standard. It is the fault of The Manager for allowing standards to fall because someone else happens to be providing that service. If The Manager has allowed that supplier to provide the service in their venue, it is The Manager's responsibility. It is right, therefore, for customers to blame the venue.

Good quality venues understand the value of their good reputation and will have a list of approved suppliers, such as caterers, which are vetted for their quality. Usually, these approved suppliers will be well-known in the industry and have a good reputation. This way, the venue has control over which company provides catering and will be confident that it will always be good quality and service to protect the reputation of the venue.

Approved suppliers can be extended to every element a venue cannot provide in-house, such as catering, furniture, floristry, decoration, disc jockeys, and marquees.

The customer can be assured that the suppliers on the venue's approved list will be good quality because no venue would include a ropey supplier. Usually, the approved suppliers are known or can easily be researched to check quality, standards,

AUTHOR'S VOICE

As a venue manager, my main role is to protect the reputation of my venue. I attend all meetings so my clients will not have any need to speak with other departments or suppliers without my knowledge. It may sound harsh and strict, but I need to be fully involved with what is being planned to happen in my venue so I can continue to protect its reputation.

Often, my clients make requests for elements I cannot approve – anything from fire hazards to naked dancers – if it risks the reputation of my venue, I will not approve it to happen.

Clients are quick to learn the way I operate so it does not take long for them to fall in line with the way I do things. In fact, they tend to respect a voice of expertise who guides them the right way to ensure the outcome of a successful and safe event.

and customer testimonials. But whenever a supplier is not known, they must be vetted. Vetting is not complicated – it is a matter of having a meeting to discuss the provision of the requirements. Even at the first meeting, it can be evident of their standards and quality by the way they present themselves and how well the relationship builds – even the terminology they use and people they know.

There are other tools to help establish the quality of a supplier, including menu tasting, visiting the supplier at another event in progress to sample their product, talking to the supplier's previous customers, and asking for a trial.

INDUSTRY VOICE

"It could be said that reputation is more important than any sales, marketing or PR. Building a strong reputation focussing on a specific target market builds loyalty.

An example is how we at Wivenhoe House dealt with the UK Government guidelines to operate during the COVID-19 pandemic. As a business we decided to follow the guidelines precisely, and in fact do more, giving our guests the comfort and confidence when visiting. As we came out of Lockdown 3, we could already see those people making reservations to return".

Oliver Brown, General Manager, Wivenhoe House Hotel

2.1 The Cost of Not Achieving Customer Satisfaction

It may sound like hard work to achieve 100% customer satisfaction. Does it really matter so much if a proportion of customers are dissatisfied with the service experience they have received?

In isolation, no, it does not really matter so much if a few customers are dissatisfied. And in the short term – today – if a customer leaves the event or hotel and is dissatisfied, it does not have a great impact.

The issue is that we cannot isolate a customer who is dissatisfied. They will leave the event or hotel with a negative experience and can freely share their negative experience about our event or hotel with their friends, other clients, other customers, on review websites and on social media platforms. If they are connected in the industry, they are free to share their negative views with people we work with – our suppliers, caterers, clients – and they can go on doing this for as long as they wish, and there is nothing The Manager can do about it. The Manager will not even know it is happening.

Multiply this scenario by the number of customers who are dissatisfied – and you may not know how many there are because they will not all complain to you, and if you are not conducting consistent and effective evaluation and feedback procedures, you will not know how many customers are dissatisfied, anyhow – and it becomes a frightening situation that will damage your business and risk its future.

Besides, there is no such thing as a short-term dissatisfied customer. For a customer to have a negative experience at an event or hotel where they expected to have an enjoyable and positive experience, because that is the perception given to them, is a psychological impact. Painful experiences linger in the memory. Dissatisfaction does not melt away from the mind of a customer just because the event has ended or their hotel stay is over.

Dissatisfaction does not disappear

It can be seen how dissatisfaction is costly because it is a web within social and socio-professional networks stretching for as long as the customer continues spinning it.

The Manager cannot do anything about it once it is in progress. The only points of control are before and during the customer experience at the event or in the hotel. This is why it is essential to ensure optimum customer service before and during the customer's arrival and maintain it until the customer's departure. And afterwards measure and check whether they were satisfied.

AUTHOR'S VOICE

I once took a client to view a venue I was proposing for their event. I took them there because it was a beautiful venue, well known, in central London.

When we arrived, the venue manager enacted the exchange of business cards between himself and my client and then we began the tour.

A day or two afterwards, my client telephoned to inform me that the venue manager had contacted them direct to offer to host their event with all the requirements including an event manager to organise everything. This would not require my services, obviously. If my client had chosen to accept this offer, I would be cut out, and the venue would have 100% of the job and a new client.

It was fortunate that this was a longstanding client of mine – we had a good relationship and she trusted me and enjoyed working with me to produce her events. Otherwise, she may have taken that offer and I might not have known why I didn't get the job.

I never took another client to that venue. I never considered it ever again – losing a client to them was too high a risk to take – so their act lost any future business I might have placed with them. But I also took pleasure to spread the word to my event network that this is how that venue operates so avoid it at all costs.

By checking afterwards, The Manager will be informed whether the customer was satisfied. If they are dissatisfied, it is still within control to recover that customer by taking action to mitigate their disappointment. It might be as simple as an acknowledgement and apology or it could require a gift basket, discount on their next visit, or a refund.

It is not knowing that a customer is dissatisfied which is damaging because if it is not known, it cannot be recovered.

If good customer service is not achieved, there are costs. First, there is the financial cost from the decrease in customers or low uptake of ticket sales, and The Manager will not know how many customers are *not* coming to the event or hotel. Customers who are not customers are unknown. They are invisible. It is therefore impossible to calculate the cost of lost business as a result of poor customer service.

Also, there is the cost of additional marketing and promotion activities in the attempt to entice new customers and fill the void of non-customers. Marketing and advertising costs money from the business, but it also requires the time and effort of a paid member of the team who could perhaps be more efficient elsewhere in the business than trying to win customers to a business with poor customer service.

Another financial cost is on the profit and loss account – the P&L – because lost business, a downturn in trade, additional marketing costs, and staff being paid to try and win business instead of serving customers will each have an impact on profit.

Remember, events and hotel rooms are perishable because once the date has gone, it cannot be resold. When the event is over, it cannot rehappen to recapture lost sales. And if hotel rooms have not sold that night, they have lost their revenue potential for that day – and that day is not going to happen again.

Lost profit cannot be regained

Other than financial costs, poor customer service has an impact on related business costs, such as reputation, discussed above. There are staffing issues as well, such as low staff morale and high turnover of staff because nobody enjoys dealing with dissatisfied customers or working in a job where customer service is not important. All costs link to profit, of course, because if staff are demotivated, they are inefficient and if they leave, it costs money from the business to replace them because of recruitment and training costs.

The Manager should remember that if staff morale is low, it will impact customer service so it becomes a downward spiral. And if there are gaps in staffing levels because of high or frequent turnover, it will impact customer service because there will be a drop in standards whilst there is a shortage of staff and whilst new recruits are trained to optimum levels of providing customer service.

It can be seen how customer service is interconnected with every other element of the event or hotel and has impacts in every area. Customer service is not only about what the customer receives. It is also about how the business performs. It goes right to the profit line and the sustained success of the event or hotel.

There is no escape from the positive impacts of good customer service and the negative impacts of poor customer service.

References

Brown, T., and Stokes, P. (2021) 'Events Management As a Community of Practice', *Journal of Hospitality and Tourism Insights*, 4(1). doi: 10.1108/JHTI-09-2020-0157.

Chapter 3

Knowing Your Customers

This chapter explores the techniques that assist businesses to understand their customers and the competition they face when trying to attract them.

Section 3.0 maps the alternatives available to current and future customers by creating a competitor analysis model to display the market.

In Section 3.1, we delve into the different methods of defining your specific target market and ways to fully understand the people who will be or already are your customers. We explain how to identify a customer persona – a fictional character who fits into your customer target range – to reach and engage with that customer type.

Section 3.2 explores personalising your offer to fit individual customers and the importance of adapting your product to fit that target. Here, we share some ideas for personalising products to suit customers and other ideas to suit sponsors. We further identify seven benefits of personalising your business to customers.

Section 3.3 discusses the merits of computerised Customer Relationship Management (CRM) systems and how they can be applied to personalise the experience of customers at hotels and events.

DOI: 10.4324/9781003154600-4

Section 3.4 identifies seven reasons why loyal customers are valuable as well as five ways to encourage loyal customers to return and to act as advocates for your business.

In Section 3.5, we discuss the power of customer referrals and the reasons for tracking the percentage source of bookings.

3.0 Knowing Your Competition

To fully understand your customer, you need to be able to look through their lens and see what they have seen prior to arriving at your door. This means knowing all the alternatives that a customer had, and either discarded or was unaware of, before purchasing your product. This knowledge will help you stay ahead of competition and prevent the situation where a customer regrets their purchase and compares you negatively against another business. Effectively, your competitor is raising the expectations of your current customer because of an experience they had elsewhere!

A common method to get a snapshot of your competition is to create a graphic that plots your competition against you in terms of quality versus price. The trick is in finding a way to measure the quality of what you offer against the price of an identical product which you are both offering. For instance, if the product is a wedding, the competition would be any venue within your catchment area that is offering a dining experience with or without a licence that actively attracts weddings.

Find an equivalent product which is similar for all the competition types, for example, a three-course basic offer with flowers, buffet, and DJ. Some of the competitors might have much better packages and some may not, but for the purpose of price comparison use a product that is broadly similar and then look through their websites to find the prices being charged.

This is your x-axis and it works best if you put these prices into categories, that is, 1 = £0.00– £5.00pp (per person), 2 = £6.00– £10.00pp, 3 = £11.00– £15.00pp, and so on to give a score from 1 to 20 for each competitor venue (Figure 3.1).

The second step is a little more difficult as you will need to find a way to measure quality in a neutral and reliable way. Many businesses would use *Tripadvisor* at this point and there is a logic to that, but the issue with this is that *Tripadvisor* measures what customers received versus their expectations, which is not measuring the actual quality. For instance, the Ritz Hotel does not score overly high on *Tripadvisor* because customers arrive with very high expectations and will expect perfection, whereas a four-star hotel might score higher because their customers are pleasantly surprised.

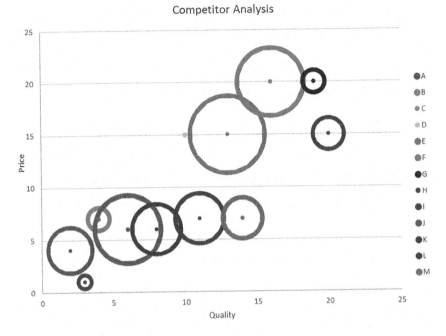

Figure 3.1 Competitor Analysis Scatter Graph

A more reliable measure, then, might be that the 25-point score (Figure 3.1) is split and includes a number of elements that make up a perfect wedding: for instance, can you get married on site; is the venue particularly photogenic with a history behind it; is there ample parking; or a good reputation for quality food; has the food won awards; have critics rated the local venues; what are the reviews like from past customers?; etc. By attributing points for each element of the wedding offer, you can build up a score out of 25 which measures quality for each competitor business and compare the two.

The third step is to measure the threat of each competitor because if a venue can only hold 20 covers, it holds minimal threat to a large conference venue regularly hosting weddings of up to 200. Conduct some research into your competitors to find their capacity and use this as a measure of the size of the competition. On the graphic adjust the size of the marker in relation to its threat. The best way to do this is by using a scatter graph on a spreadsheet where you can enlarge each marker in relation to each other (but there is nothing stopping you doing this by hand if you prefer).

We can immediately see from looking at Figure 3.1 that this is a competitive market with quite a few competitors (labelled A–M) with a range of prices (the x-axis meaning the higher up the bubble, the more expensive) and quality scores (the further along the y-axis, the higher the quality) as well as the level of threat (the size of the bubble).

Whenever this exercise is conducted there tends to be no businesses in either the top-left or bottom-right corner of the scatter graph. This makes sense as the top-left would be a high price option with poor quality and would receive negative feedback, whereas the bottom-right would be great quality at a low price and probably not viable.

If our business is L in the middle, we are in quite a precarious position with businesses all around us of higher and lower quality with both higher and lower prices.

The biggest threat would be K to the left of us because that business is currently offering a similar quality product at a cheaper price, whereas M is offering weddings at a higher price but the same quality and could be a target for us to take some market share.

This exercise is a useful one as it helps you to visualise what the customer does before choosing a venue for their wedding. They will likely visit multiple competitors before making their decision and it is important to know where you sit amongst the competition to ensure you are not overpriced and losing business but also open to negative feedback if the customer believes that they could have got a better deal elsewhere.

It is also a useful exercise to look for ways to improve your quality and thereby your position amongst the competition. If for instance you did not have a wedding licence to marry onsite, or had an option to extend parking, you could replot the graphic with your new score and make a judgement on whether the expense would bring a return.

Furthermore, it encourages you to keep an eye on the competition and continually update the graphic. For instance, a venue that offers a special deal can easily be repositioned and the threat reanalysed. Another that refurbished their ballroom or extended it can similarly be monitored instantly.

Once satisfied that our business has a place in the market and is not compromised, we can move on to the target market and its characteristics.

3.1 Knowing Your Target Market

Event businesses do not have just one type of customer. They have ranges of customers who are very different depending on the product(s) on offer. For example, a comedy night will attract a different customer to an ABBA tribute act, say. Likewise, a day conference differs from a children's birthday party. Their expectations, needs, wishes, and demands will all be different. It may sound obvious but knowing the customer type for each of the products being offered by the venue is very important as customers will each need to be handled in different ways.

There are many accepted theoretical methods to define markets using socio-economic banding (putting customers into categories depending on their wealth) or behavioural segmentation (defining customers by personality and buying behaviour) or just by geography, for instance. However, a more modern method of quantifying customers in hotels is to create a persona for each product. This is creating a fictional character who fits squarely in the middle of the target customer range. It can be developed using past history or by tracking enquiries, or often just by common sense.

For instance, if the target market for the ABBA tribute act is customers 30–50 years of age, with a household income range of between £30,000 and £50,000 and is mostly female, a possible persona might be the profile of the target customer in Figure 3.2:

The reason this method is becoming widely used is because it simplifies the thought process when deciding how to reach and engage that customer. For example, marketers would now ask themselves what does Sandie read; which social media site does she visit the most; what does she look for in a website? What is important to her when she arrives; when she buys a drink or goes through security? Should we adapt the toilets for the night to avoid queues? Is there enough room to dance or have we sold too many tickets to allow that to happen?

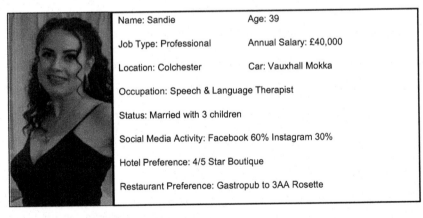

Figure 3.2 Fictional Customer Persona

"Creating personas for each of our products was such an eye-opener and changed our marketing strategy.

In the past we would have advertised on similar platforms and using similar magazines, etc. for every product.

Personas helped us personalise the messages and how they were directed to the customer. It also helped us to understand the customer and create some unique selling points (USPs)!"

Adam Rowledge, Managing Director, Rowledge Associates

3.2 Personalising Your Offer

Knowing your customer will allow you to predict potential issues with your product in advance as well as find the best ways to attract customers through marketing initiatives.

It also allows you to get into the mindset of the customer and begin tailoring and personalising your offer.

Customers have become used to being targeted through personalised products, from McDonalds allowing the option of customised orders to latte coffees with low-fat sprinkles, almond milk, and whipped cream.

Hotels and events have long adapted to customised services and products to meet their customers' desires and needs. At a time long past, hotels were hostelries for food, drink, and a bed for weary travellers, and even provided stables for their customers' horses! As needs and wants changed, the services changed with it – they still do, with things like décor, technology, and new trends. Hotels have diversified their services to meet their customers' tastes but also to attract more trade by providing bars, gin bars and cocktail bars, cafes, different styles of restaurants, casinos, afternoon tea, meeting rooms, conference spaces, and ballrooms.

Events have adapted, too. Nowadays they cater to attendees and audiences who have experienced events before and have evolved their expectations. So, events have become more creative and complex. A notable development in events is their shift from hotels to other venues such as country houses, castles, libraries, art galleries, museums, and disused warehouses.

It is all about personalising the offer to attract customers – even when there are thousands of tickets being sold. This should not be viewed as adding complexity: more often it is adding potential revenue streams because offering personalised products can charge a fee and premium fees. For instance, music festivals attract a multitude of customers from students on low funds to celebrities with unlimited budgets. Should the festival just have one ticket price for all attendees to make it less complex, or would it not make sense to give as many options as possible and let the customer decide if they want to pay the extra for premium services? Often, providing extra options incurs no expense to the business at all.

Example – a music festival with 10,000 capacity can sell either:

10,000 tickets at £50.00 per person = £500,000 revenue

Or

7,000 tickets at £50.00pp

1,000 tickets with early access and ability to pitch their tent nearer the stages at + £25.00pp

1,000 tickets with priority parking for easier departure + £25.00pp

500 tickets with early access to performances for front-of-stage views + £25.00pp

500 VIP tickets at £500.00pp with backstage passes + £100.00pp

None of the above extras incur further costs to the festival, other than administration, and yet this example would generate an additional £67,500 income.

Here are some further ideas for personalising the offer to customers:

- Access to VIP areas
- Meet and Greet the performer, artist, singer, celebrity
- Ticket denominations – standing; seated; balcony; front of stage; side of stage; private box; VIP; early access

- Early purchase discount ('early-bird')

- Loyalty discount for repeat purchase (if the customer has purchased before or is purchasing at this event for a future event)

- Ticket inclusions – merchandise; signed merchandise; goodie bag; drinks package; dining

- Car service door-to-door

And here are some ideas for personalising sponsors' packages:

- Pre-event reception or a post-event reception

- Tables to host their customers or friends at the event; private dining area

- Premium seating

- Hospitality room or area for the sponsor to meet and socialise with their guests

- Company name and logo included in marketing collateral; onstage branding

- Company name and logo in the title of the event (this would be the 'title sponsor' or 'headline sponsor' such as the "BRIT Awards with MasterCard")

Note: Sponsors which are offered smaller packages would be 'satellite sponsors' of which there could be two, three, or many. Each might receive a condensed version of the title sponsor's package or a range of versions depending on their sponsorship level – a low sponsorship level might only receive tickets to the event, say.

Businesses need to be looking for ways to personalise wherever they can to enjoy the following benefits:

1 Customers will willingly pay extra to receive a product that is slightly superior to the norm. Many customers like to feel special and be picked out of a crowd for special treatment – especially if they are bringing with them friends or family. It is about giving differentiated products that are available to everyone, but only received by those who are willing to pay for it.

2 Personalisation can generate additional profits and sales if the differentiated product is superior to competitors, and if the product can be adapted using current systems and staffing it can often be pure profit.

3 Personalised products can give you a unique selling point (USP) because competitor events or hotels are not offering these or cannot offer them. This will enable you to compete with higher quality products.

4 Often the product itself is still the same, and it is just being creative with add-ons and knowing your customers' frustrations and wants to be creative with the offer.

5   By watching sales trends, it will actually give you an insight in to the customer, for instance if one package starts to sell out, it is a sign that this is something missing from your original product or maybe is on trend at the moment.

6   Being harder to copy is always a good thing and personalising products is a good way to improve loyalty as customers with diverse needs appreciate businesses that go out of their way to adapt to them.

7   The online element to most purchases means your options are immediately visible to the customer at the point of booking and can be very attractive to discerning customers.

3.3 Customer Relationship Management

An effective way of evolving relationships with customers is through the application of a computerised CRM system. These systems are technology-based and are usually part of a wider front-office software package such as bookings and guest relations systems. Such systems have improved over recent years but their origins are in 'guest history' whereby a hotel can track a customer's previous stay and maintain a record of their likes, dislikes, and purchase history. These systems provide a snapshot of each customer so that when they return, the hotel knows a lot about them and can personalise their services to meet the desires of that customer. This means that as soon as the customer checks-in and the receptionist opens their booking record, this customer's guest history will be visible, down to the receptionist knowing whether the customer prefers to be called Mr Berners, Philip, or Phil. We will know what room the customer previously occupied and whether he likes that same room. Or, he might like a balcony room or a top-floor room. We will know whether he likes champagne, red wine, or white wine, and we can also record any other details which would make future stays more comfortable for this guest.

A CRM system allows staff to personalise their service to each customer for familiarity and it will also help the customer to slip seamlessly into the hotel without the need for questions such as would they like a morning newspaper and which they prefer.

Personal details of a guest can be recorded as well such as their birth date, their spouse's name, their children's names, and where they live. These details facilitate the returning-welcome so that the receptionist or The Manager can greet the guest and enquire about his family and his journey today.

But a CRM system is not just for niceties and familiarities. It is also a marketing tool to engage with customers with certain preferences. If the hotel is doing a promotion of a stay-and-dine package, say, the CRM database can select all guests who have used the restaurant during their stay to reach that target market.

Due to the costs of technology and the installation or upgrade of computerised systems, event organisers are less likely to purchase a CRM system. This is justified because events are temporary one-off live happenings and do not require guest histories to be kept to the extent of a hotel with returning guests. The main difference here is that a hotel needs to maintain a continued relationship with their customers, whereas an event quite often will not have that need.

However, the benefits of a computerised CRM system are clear to see for events because it can track client preferences as well as attendee histories. It is helpful to know, for instance, the background of an attendee to understand their purchase history, are they a returning attendee, do they spend at the bar?, etc. But most event organisers will rely on a customer database system as a hybrid version of a full CRM system (unless the event organiser is employed at a venue or hotel with a computerised CRM system).

3.4 Customer Loyalty

Customer loyalty is where somebody repeatedly buys a product or service because of their belief in either the brand or the business, or the product itself.

It can be simply repeating a purchase but could also be so strong that customers actively tell their friends and family about your product and encourage them to buy it, too. This is obviously highly desirable:

1   Repeat customers tend to spend more; they are less cautious and highly familiar with the options available to them and hence are willing and confident to spend more to get more.

2   The chance of succeeding with an offer or advertising campaign is much higher with repeat customers and so a mailshot (letter or email to past customers with a 'unique' offer) can help you sell out at quiet times if required.

3   Repeat customers are on your database so are already an identified (and often engaging) target market.

4   It is expensive to attract new customers and you never know when they might bring with them unrealistic expectations.

5   Marketing to new customers is ad hoc and you do not know how many hit the mark or reach the right people who will engage. This is why blanket marketing occurs – to reach as wide a demographic as possible – but can have proportionately limited results.

6   Either naturally or with incentives, repeat customers can promote your business for you, maybe so much so, there is no longer a need to advertise (organic marketing).

7   Repeat customers who become known or familiar can provide you with honest and valuable feedback on your business and service, not just from a one-off perspective but also from a long-term angle.

Loyal customers will occur naturally if you are meeting and exceeding the expectations of your customers. However, many businesses have found innovative and creative ways to encourage customers to return and to act as advocates (actively promoting the business externally):

1   Rewards programmes, offering incentives to return such as every fifth event you attend the sixth is free, or free items for regular visits. If this is tied to memorabilia for instance it can help push customers to advocate status.

2   Referrals, where bringing in a new customer by recommendation is rewarded in some way with special treatment, discounts, or freebies. Keep in mind that if you are achieving business through an online travel agent (OTA), you might be losing 20%–30% of your revenue each booking and this allows you to give a substantial reward to an advocate without losing profit (as long as the new customer books direct).

3   Ensure staff are well trained and motivated to deal with issues and complaints so you will not lose loyal customers. Remember, if a complaint is dealt with well, it can create a loyal customer despite the error (see Chapter 7, *Dealing with Complaints*).

4   Loyalty cards and identifiers are great ways to collect data on customers' buying habits and tailor your offers and freebies to each advocate while recording valuable data on them.

5   Have a commitment to quality in everything you do and employ staff who believe in this and will go out of their way for your customers.

3.5 Customer Referrals

For a customer to receive advertising through the recommendation of a friend or colleague who has already purchased the product is very powerful. It removes the worry that advertisers might be exaggerating their product or service. It allows a friend to ask questions of the purchaser and the answers are delivered by someone they trust.

Customers actively look for recommendations – even from strangers on review sites and are often willing to alter their purchasing behaviour because of a review.

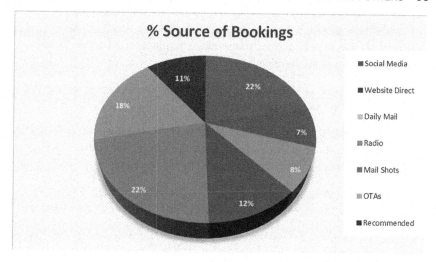

Figure 3.3 Percentage Source of Bookings

If customers are this easily swayed, imagine how powerful an advocate can be for your business.

Most businesses track the source of their bookings like the report above (Figure 3.3):

Some of the above advertising methods cost money to the business and take away hard-earned profits, particularly the online booking fee. The recommendations (referrals) are of course free and yet in this example bring in 11% of the business which is greater than the Daily Mail advert, for instance. Therefore, ensuring satisfaction of customers has a dual impact: it increases loyalty and return custom as well as increasing recommendations.

Many businesses simply allow loyalty to occur naturally and enjoy the benefits from it. But loyalty should be actively promoted and rewards given to loyal customers as a marketing technique to their benefit but at minimal cost to the business.

AUTHOR'S VOICE

Although the benefits of loyal customers are important and valuable, The Manager should be careful because they do not know what has been said and what the expectations are.

I recommended a restaurant to a colleague. I have eaten there on numerous occasions with friends, family, and even with my clients. I have each time received consistent good food and excellent service – otherwise I would not have recommended this place, and I certainly would not have returned there with my clients!

Yet, my colleague did not enjoy her experience when she visited this restaurant on my recommendation.

Maybe this was because of her own level of expectation, or her personal tastes, or that she had a negative mindset that day – she might have had an argument with her boyfriend – I don't know!

It was only a little awkward for me. I reiterated to her that I always had a good time at that restaurant and tried to uphold my recommendation.

But, thinking from The Manager's perspective, they would not have known that this customer had been referred, or by whom, or what had been said to them. Maybe, I oversold it to my colleague and unrealistically raised her expectations?

You can see how difficult it is for a manager to provide their product, quality, and service to what I had said to my colleague.

I suppose it could have been an 'off' night for the restaurant. Maybe the head chef was not there or there was a change in staff? This is always the risk when recommending a restaurant.

The *only* solution is to provide consistent high quality of service to all customers whether they are new, returning, or have been referred. This will not only be good for business, but it will prevent people like me from hesitating to make a recommendation!

Chapter **4**

Know Your Promise to the Customer

This chapter dissects the idiom *'the customer is always right'* to determine whether it is true. We then look at what we are promising to our customers and how to align your offer to meet customer expectations.

Section 4.1 identifies what you can deliver to customers by segmenting each aspect of what you are offering and then analysing each segment and sub-segment to determine if you are honestly delivering the right level of expectations.

With Section 4.2, we look at how to set customer expectations without the dishonesty of over-promising, so that alignment is achieved with expectations being set and expectations being met.

In Section 4.3, we take an in-depth look at customer perception of hotels through the use of hotel brands and sub-brands (Section 4.3.1) in attracting customer-specific interest and engagement. This serves to target individual consumer groups who are interested in one side of the service but not others so as to avoid marketing fatigue through blanket marketing to disinterested customers. In this section, we discuss the merits of hotel marketing consortia (Section 4.3.2) in creating customer perception of member hotels but we also identify customer confusion with hotel consortia. We then expose the myths of the hotel star rating system (Section 4.3.3) which persists in being misperceived by hotel customers. We visit online booking systems (Section 4.3.4) and their influence with

DOI: 10.4324/9781003154600-5

Electronic Word of Mouth (EWORM) and then we offer a brief evaluation of hotel accreditation bodies (Section 4.3.5).

Section 4.4 moves us into the events arena where we look at engaging with customer perceptions through the senses – experiential events – and how setting objectives (Section 4.4.1) allows The Manager to measure their performance in meeting customer satisfaction targets. Here, we outline the need for Key Performance Indicators (KPIs) to track performance during the planning of an event and for measuring actual performance against objectives after an event has happened.

4.0 Is the Customer Always Right?

No. The customer is not always right. Of course, they're not. So, how did this idiom come to exist, that the customer is always right.

The Manager *wants* the customer to be right. We all want our customers to be right. But this is an ideology and whilst it is helpful to keep in mind when dealing with customers or their complaints, it does not mean that customers *are* always right.

Closer to reality is this:

The customer is right in expecting to receive the expectations given to them.

If the customer has been given expectations of the experience they are going to receive – it could be the level of service; the quality of food or accommodation; the fun experience they will receive by attending this event – whatever it is that has been promised to them, if they then do not receive the experience to meet their expectations, they are right not to be happy about that.

It is not the customer's fault if they have not received the level of expectation that was given to them by the event or hotel.

It is not their fault that The Manager did not achieve to meet that level of expectation.

The Manager sets the expectations of the customer. This is what the customer expects to receive and what they expect The Manager to deliver. If the service they experience fails to meet their expectations, that is the fault of The Manager. Which is why the customer is always right.

If The Manager did not intend to set that level of expectation to the customer, it is still the fault of The Manager because expectations should be set to the capability of the service being promised to customers.

If the customer chooses to attend this event or visit this hotel – if they have spent time considering what has been promised to them, and have then decided to spend their money on that service, plus the costs of travelling to get there – if they pay for this through their choice, they deserve to receive what they have paid for. Which is why the customer is always right.

The Manager intends to deliver the best service to customers. That is understandable. But if promising something to a customer which cannot be given, it is not delivering the best. In fact, it is dishonest.

So, be honest – what can you deliver?

INDUSTRY VOICE

"As General Manager, I closed the Beverley Hills Sun Inter-Continental Hotel in Umhlanga Rocks, near Durban in South Africa for a significant refurbishment project. But we had to reopen in time for The Rothmans Durban July Handicap horserace on the first Saturday in July. Then, we could showcase our fantastic new 5-star hotel to the great and the good from Johannesburg who come to Durban for this big race.

The only problem was that we did not have the hotel ready on time, and the complaints were numerous from guests whom we were desperate to impress.

One complaint which remains vivid in my mind to this day were a family who arrived and had booked interconnecting rooms. One room was ready, but one wasn't. We explained this to the family and said that they could check-in to the room that was ready and we would let them know in a while when the other room was ready.

Our mistake however was in not locking the interconnecting door. The father decided to open it to see what state the room was in, only to find a decorator still hanging the wallpaper!

I don't think they paid for their rooms that night and I still break into nervous sweats 25 years later just thinking about that weekend".

Andrew Coggings, Managing Director of Hospitality, The Goodwood Estate

4.1 What Can You Deliver?

Begin by segmenting each aspect of what you are offering to your customers.

For a hotel it might be:

- **Quality**
  - Bedrooms
  - Front of house areas
  - Restaurants
  - Bars
  - Food
  - Drink
  - Entertainment
- **Service**
  - Pre-arrival communication and preparation
  - Reception/Check-in/Check-out
  - Staff service
  - Room service
  - Housekeeping service
  - In-room service
  - Food and drink service
  - After-departure follow-up and evaluation
- **Décor**
  - Good standard and maintenance of decoration
  - Use of recent photos and images
  - Use of summer and winter images
  - Use of realistic images (not corrected, filtered, or stretched to alter the size of spaces or rooms)
- **Ambience**
  - Lighting
  - Colours

- Mood
- Style of music and sound levels
- Style of establishment
- **Facilities**
  - Spa
  - Gym
  - Leisure (tennis, squash, golf, swimming)
  - Conference, banqueting, or event spaces
  - Event manager or wedding planner
  - Bars and restaurants
  - In-room facilities

Then analyse each of the segments and sub-segments identified within your offer to your customer. Is the message being given to your customers honestly delivering the right level of expectations when they arrive and partake in the service on offer?

It seems a difficult and laborious task. But it is the job of The Manager to do this because it is about setting the expectations of customers so they are happy with the service when they receive it.

It is about understanding the business by analysing what is being offered to the customer against what the customer expects to receive.

And it is a great thing to do; to understand the business and the customers being invited to spend their money with you so that the business makes profit. There is nothing difficult or laborious about that. It should be a joy to do.

There are generic segments which fit with hotels and events – which are each providing hospitality services to customers:

- Quality
- Service
- Décor
- Ambience
- Facilities

But events are short-term live happenings and they are changeable, so the sub-segments will change with the style and nature of each event. A business conference will differ in sub-segments from a music festival, for example.

With events the pre-event planning stage sets the expectations to the customer. So, whatever is being planned for, the event needs to deliver to the expectations of the attendee:

- Marketing
  - Customer reach (communications, PR, social media)
  - Invitation type, style, wording
- Purpose of event
  - Why attend (fun, thrill, networking, knowledge)
  - What the attendee will receive when they attend
  - Benefits of attending
  - What the attendee will lose out on if they do not attend
- Content of event
  - How much it will cost
  - What is included in the price
  - What experience they will receive
  - What they will gain (learning; knowledge; networking; an amazing experience)
- After the event
  - Will they receive loyalty discount for the next event
  - Will they have the opportunity to provide feedback of their experience
  - Will they receive future opportunities such as first-release ticket options

Then analyse each of the segments and sub-segments identified within the offer to the customer. Is the message being given to potential customers honestly delivering the right level of expectations when the customer arrives to the event and partakes in the experience you are offering?

4.2 Setting Customer Expectations

Setting expectations can be quite easy. If you are honest. Honest with yourself and your customers.

The Manager needs to think about what the business is offering the customer if they decide to attend the event or visit the hotel.

Although The Manager might have aspirations to offer the very best, be honest in understanding whether it is the best being offered and is able to be delivered. Otherwise, it will build customer expectations and then let them down.

The trick to achieve customer success is to set standards that meet customer expectations.

AUTHOR'S VOICE

I would expect McDonalds to meet customer expectations better than the Ritz Hotel.

This is because the Ritz Hotel has created the promise of the highest levels of customer service which is rightly the expectation of a guest who can afford to stay at the Ritz.

Raising customer expectations to this degree is difficult to meet in practice (although the Ritz has perfected customer service and delivers it very well) so customers are likely to complain if they spot anything which does not meet that exacting standard.

When visiting McDonalds, however, a customer does not have the expectation of five-star standards. A customer at McDonalds expects what to receive, and McDonalds is the exemplar of providing that consistent standard.

Both the Ritz Hotel and McDonalds are expert at delivering what the customer expects to receive. But at each, their customers have a different level of expectation of what they will receive. So, as long as that expectation is delivered, there will be no complaints whether it is a luxury hotel stay or a burger and fries.

A customer is not going to expect the highest standards of facilities if you do not sell that idea to them. Budget hotels sell the promise of quick, efficient, and affordable accommodation without promising butler service, fine dining restaurants, and luxury suites. This enables the budget hotel to deliver on the promise they are creating and selling. There is a target market for budget hotels which reaches and attracts the type of customer who is expecting quick, efficient, and affordable accommodation and will not be disappointed when they receive that service. Budget hotels do this very well – they are still clean, comfortable, and friendly places to stay; it is just that they set expectations to their target market.

Think about how the customer is going to perceive your business. They may visit the website or look at the brochure. They might receive information about the event or hotel through social media channels or review websites.

The marketing you create is the beginning of setting the customer's expectations of that event or hotel.

Problems occur with promising the best and not being able to deliver it.

It is a professional mistake to over-promise if you cannot deliver on that promise. It would be raising the level of expectation that will not be met. This is where the Ritz Hotel gets it right because they promise highly and have to deliver to it. Can your event or hotel do that?

If the promise does not meet the expectations of customers, they will be right in feeling disappointed; cheated; misled. A false representation has been created to achieve their business, and that is dishonest.

Some businesses do this on purpose – they will promise something which they know they cannot deliver but at least it gets tickets sold and customers through the door. It is unethical, of course.

Whichever it is – intentional unethical practice or simply the mistake of mis-aligned customer expectations – if a customer is dissatisfied they will complain.

It should be noted that it can be a mix of intentionally misleading customers and unintentional customer dissatisfaction because some businesses will promise something but deliver something else. An example would be 'loss-leader' promotions where a business offers something to entice customers into the hotel or event, and then once they are captured, delivers something else or additional.

This is where the practice of upselling and cross-selling nears the territory of being unethical. It is acceptable practice to upsell to enhance a customer's experience whilst increasing spend and profit. But if the customer does not want it or does not know about it, it becomes unethical practice. An example of this would be a service charge added to the bill: if the customer did not want to pay for service or they were unaware they were being charged for service, it is unethical practice.

Setting expectations may be relatively easy to do, but the difficulty is that The Manager is not always in control of doing so. A lot of the expectations a customer perceives arrive from a range of diverse sources beyond the control of The Manager.

This means that The Manager will not always be aware of each customer's expectations – if they have received their expectations from what other people have said (word of mouth), or social media chatter, a referral, or recommendation, The Manager will not know what has been said to the customer, nor how the customer has interpreted what was said.

However, if The Manager is running a good business and is paying close attention to these social channels, they would be able to closely reflect what is being provided to customers, which is a good thing.

It is important to ensure that the correct expectations are being delivered by those channels which are within the control of The Manager such as the website or brochure, marketing blurb, or marketing campaign. By carefully placing the marketing collateral to deliver the right customer expectations helps with the peripheral channels that are not within the control of The Manager. This can be done by cross-aligning channels of communication so that if a customer is told what a great event this will be or what a wonderful hotel to visit, they can check for themselves by visiting your website, obtaining your brochure, or scanning the social media platforms and review sites.

By doing this, The Manager can make some headway in regulating or tempering a customer's expectations. In the same way that a Manager may respond to a negative review to inform customers that this negative aspect is not a true likeness of their service, The Manager can align glowing reviews with what is actual about their business.

Naturally, a Manager is unlikely to want to water down a glowing review once it has been gratefully received. Some managers might actively encourage inflated reviews by posting them themselves, asking their staff to post them, or enrolling friends and family to do so. But this goes against that ethos of aligning customer expectations with the reality of the service they will receive, so will only lead to disappointment and short-lived gain. However, to expect a Manager to refute a glowing review is a stretch. But the point here is for The Manager to be aware of what the reviews are saying about the business – and if they are glowing testimonials, the business needs to glow with them to ensure the next customer receives that same high level of service and quality.

The Manager must reflect and consider what message – what expectation – is being channelled to customers that will set their level of expectation. The logo being used, the invitation being sent, the look of the event, venue, or hotel – every part of what the customer sees delivers a perception of expectation.

If there is going to be disparity with setting expectations and the service experience a customer receives, The Manager should err on the side of underselling. That is, lowering the level of expectations so the customer is pleasantly surprised.

It may not be the ideal solution to undersell because the optimum level of customer satisfaction will be achieved when there is alignment with expectations being given and expectations being met. But underselling is better than overselling because it is better to delight the customer with service greater than expected rather than disappoint them by not delivering the service they expected.

4.3 Customer Perception of Hotels

A lot of customer perceptions for a hotel are clear to interpret. Customers are aware that a five-star luxury hotel delivers high-quality standards which is not the same perception as a budget hotel delivering functionality, speed, and simplicity.

One is not better than the other – they both deliver what is promised. Nor is it that one has better standards and quality than another. A budget hotel and a five-star hotel both provide the highest level of standards and quality for that sector of the hospitality industry – this is what the customer expects. A customer would not expect a budget hotel to have unlaundered sheets and an unclean bathroom just because it is not a five-star luxury hotel and costs less.

The difference, then, is not in quality, standards, cleanliness, hygiene, or safety but in the perception of what the customer expects from the type of hotel they are booking.

Hotel organisations are aware of this which is why their marketing collateral is designed for the expectations of their respective target markets. Take a moment to look at the websites of a luxury hotel and a budget hotel and notice the differences. The message from each website delivers expectations to the customer so that the customer knows what is being offered (or promised) and what they should expect to receive.

It is straightforward for hotels to deliver perceptions to their customers because they are fixed premises. The style of hotel alone – beach resort hotel; country house hotel; boutique hotel; city centre hotel – determines expectations to the customer. As do the location, price, size, and facilities. The sector within which the hotel sits, sets expectations as well – budget hotel; mid-range hotel; boutique hotel; luxury hotel.

Price is one of the key influencers of customer perception. What the customer is asked to pay sets an expectation of the services they will receive and the quality. It is important that the price level fits within the pricing parameters of that sector of the market. If the price of a room is higher than another in the same sector and same location, a customer will expect something more for their money, and it raises the level of their expectation.

Of course, a hotel might decide to lower their prices to below competitor hotels in the same sector and location as a way of attracting customers. But it must be remembered that price equals expectation. So, if the price is lower, it can devalue the hotel and customers might be dissuaded from booking the cheaper hotel because their expectation of its service and quality will be lower.

With hotels, the message can be more consistent over a much longer time frame than an event would be – events are temporary. This longevity makes it imperative for hotels to set their standards for engaging with customers so that perception and expectation are met at the right level. There is a diverse range of tools available for a hotel to convey customer expectations such as guides, website, pricing policy, images being used, reviews, enquiry and booking procedures, reputation and word of mouth, and even the style of menu being offered.

4.3.1 Hotel Brands

Hotels have developed brand identity to achieve closer perceptions to their customers by further segmenting target markets into smaller more targetable consumer groups. The reputation of a hotel brand and a customer's previous experiences of using that hotel brand create expectations. Examples include Premier Inn, Travelodge, Marriott, Hilton, and Intercontinental.

Within these hotel brands are sub-brands which serve to convey differentials to customers and further meet their expectations: InterContinental Hotel Group (IHG), for instance, has 16 sub-brands in their portfolio, and Marriott has 30 sub-brands across four sectors of 'luxury', 'premium', 'select', and 'longer stays'.

An independent hotel can achieve the same effect by creating sub-brands of services within the hotel to target individual consumer groups who are customers of one side of the service and not others. It does not seem effective for a hotel with a wide range of services to blanket-market to all potential consumers, many of whom are not interested in all the services a hotel may offer. This is untargeted, speculative, and hit and miss. It could also dissuade potential consumers who receive an impression of the hotel which does not fit their requirements.

The events service of a hotel is a good example. Here, the hotel – let's call it Seaview Hotel – can create a sub-brand to target potential customers who book events into hotels. The sub-brand could be Seaview Events and would be designed to meet the interests and needs of event customers. By creating a sub-brand for Seaview Events, event customers are directed to the area of the business which is their interest such as technical specifications, room capacities, hire rates, equipment, and catering. These are services a weekend leisure guest would not be interested to find.

If our Seaview Hotel has a beautiful terrace serving afternoon tea, it could be branded Seaview Terrace Teas. This sub-brand would be designed to target consumers interested in visiting for afternoon tea but are not interested in overnight accommodation or event specifications.

Think about how a customer perceives the above sub-brands at our Seaview Hotel. They will instantly identify with the area of the business which is their interest. They are directed to the information which is specific for their interest. They can speak with a team member within that sub-brand such as the Seaview Events coordinator or the Seaview Terrace Teas supervisor without first having to speak with a receptionist or get passed around until they land with the right staff member.

By working semi-autonomously, each sub-brand can identify with their customers so that the marketing collateral targets that consumer group. Each sub-brand can build their customer-specific database for special offers and promotions with the knowledge that the customers on that database are interested in that service.

It can be seen that segmenting the wide range of services of a hotel to specific sub-brands for individual stakeholder groups is much more targeted to reach those interested customers. Otherwise, there is a range of blanket messages going to all stakeholder groups many of whom will not be interested in those other services.

There is the problem of marketing fatigue. This is where customers tire of receiving marketing messages that are irrelevant or of no interest. After some time, the customer will either routinely ignore and delete these messages or unsubscribe.

Sub-branding narrows the number of marketing messages a customer receives because if they are an afternoon tea customer but not a bedroom customer, they would not receive all the marketing messages relating to overnight stays. The customer is therefore less likely to experience marketing fatigue and will likely pay more attention to the afternoon tea marketing messages because that is their interest and it might be an offer they will uptake.

This is important because the social behaviour of consumers is moving fast with rapid advances in technology. Society moves quicker and thinks quicker. People are quicker to dismiss or reach boredom thresholds. It is quick and easy to delete, swipe, and reject messages which are repeated or uninteresting. Where the source of messages is known – such as from an event that a customer once attended or a hotel they once stayed at – they are likely to be routinely rejected and treated as unimportant or junk mail.

4.3.2 Hotel Marketing Consortia

Hotel consortia serve the purpose of strategic marketing their member hotels to target markets of customers with expectations of hotels belonging to that consortium such as Best Western, Relais & Chateaux, Small Luxury Hotels of the World, and Pride of Britain.

Member hotels pay a fee to belong to a consortium, but they must fit the criteria determined by the consortium. Member hotels are not owned or managed by a consortium. Each hotel benefits from collective marketing and promotion activities, pooled marketing resources, and the prestige and reputation of being a member hotel. This all helps set expectations to customers and to reach and engage with customers.

There is customer misperception of hotel consortia, however. People working within the hotel industry understand the concept of hotel marketing consortia. Outside the hotel industry, customers are confused and see the consortium name as a hotel brand. Customers also view a hotel belonging to a consortium as an accreditation, which is fine if the consortium is well managed and controlled, and all member hotels uphold high standards and quality.

> ### AUTHOR'S VOICE
>
> I have often heard hotel customers use the consortium name and not the hotel name, which evidences their confusion of what a hotel consortium does. They tend to think that the consortium runs the hotel.
>
> I know one person who didn't want to book a hotel because it had the consortium brand and they had previously stayed at another hotel in that consortium which they hadn't enjoyed.

There are benefits for a hotel to join a consortium for wider reach to potential customers, more powerful marketing campaigns because of pooled resources and higher budgets, and shared marketing costs. An independent hotel does not have these advantages. If the consortium is well managed and controlled, it should benefit each member hotel.

If there are too many hotels within the consortium, it becomes harder to control and manage, and some of those hotels will vary in standards and quality. This can affect other member hotels and be detrimental for the individual hotel.

4.3.3 Star Rating

The Automobile Association (AA) introduced the star rating system in 1912 to classify hotels along motoring routes their members would take. In providing perceptions of hotels to customers, a star-rated system seems like a good idea. But the opposite has happened because the star rating system has created customer misperceptions of the hotel industry.

The public mistakenly believe that the star rating of a hotel relates to quality and standards. In fact, the star rating system relates to the facilities a hotel can offer.

A hotel which offers 24-hr butler service, a fully equipped gym, and swimming pool will achieve a higher star rating for the facilities it provides than a hotel which does not have that range of facilities to offer. The misperception has occurred because a hotel that is able to offer all the facilities to achieve five stars would usually be a high-quality hotel – hence the misperception of stars relating to quality.

However, a beautiful and high-quality boutique hotel or country house hotel cannot achieve a five-star rating if they cannot provide all the facilities that meet the criteria of five stars such as air-conditioning in bedrooms or a swimming pool. Most country house hotels are historic buildings of architectural interest so they cannot install air-conditioning which means five stars are beyond their reach.

The system would work well if the customer understands stars are awarded for facilities, not standards, and that the more facilities a hotel can offer should mean it is a high-quality hotel (but that is not what the stars are awarded for).

In frequent attempts to redress the misperception it has created, the AA has played around with accreditations for quality and service, such as rosettes, diamonds, red diamonds, and yellow stars, but this has further confused the customer. The more variants there are, the more difficult it is for the customer to interpret and understand. Besides, it has not removed the original problem of the star rating misperception which persists.

4.3.4 Online Review Sites/OTAs/Online Booking Sites

Review sites, Online Travel Agents (OTAs), and online booking sites have emerged as a valuable tool in creating customer expectations.

AUTHOR'S VOICE

I know of one hotel which decided to opt out of the AA star rating scheme because one criterion of assessment was to offer morning newspapers delivered to guest bedrooms.

The hotel repeatedly asked guests if they would like a morning newspaper, but it was routinely refused because nowadays, guests read online news magazines, newsfeeds, or news apps.

This hotel felt that it was increasingly out of step to offer printed newspapers to guests and was incompatible with the hotel's eco initiatives.

Instead of being forced to continually ask guests if they would like a newspaper just so the hotel could achieve their AA star rating, they decided it was easier to opt out of the AA rating system rather than lose a star because they no longer offered newspapers to guests.

Customers leave online reviews of their experience at a hotel, and it has become usual for other customers to check online reviews during their process of decision-making. This is known as Electronic Word of Mouth (EWORM) and is valuable for a hotel to reach a wider audience of potential customers. If reviews are good, it can drive business to the hotel which otherwise it would not reach.

Because a hotel is not in control of what their customers post online about their experience, hotels have to ensure that their guests are happy (otherwise they may get a negative review). It should therefore drive hotel standards higher because hotels are aiming for great reviews. It is limited control, though, because it is difficult to please every guest – especially if the guest has not complained to the hotel but goes on to leave a negative review. There is also the issue of illegitimate reviews posted by a competitor hotel or somebody who has a grudge such as a former staff member. There are also false positive reviews which serve to inflate the reputation of a hotel and are written by friends, family, paid-for reviews, and sponsored reviewers.

Hoteliers do pay attention to EWORM because it is a powerful and very public window into the hotel's services and standards. If there are negative reviews, it creates a negative perception which has the power to drive customers away to competitor hotels and could have serious detriment to the business.

Research shows that customers vary in their attention to EWORM. Some may take a cursory glance at online reviews before they make their decision to book but do not allow the reviews to influence their decision. Some decide to book and then check reviews to reinforce their purchasing decision. Others might not rely on online reviews at all and view it as a waste of time because they are not trustworthy.

4.3.5 Hotel Accreditation

Customers can gain their perception of a hotel from accreditation bodies which provide trustful reviews and guides, such as AA, Michelin Guide, Square Meal, and VisitBritain.

Although online reviews are replacing traditional review organisations, largely because of their wider reach and broader range of reviews, there is still some weight in trustful reviews that are not consumer-led or reviewed by customers who are wont to be fickle with their likes and dislikes and may not be justified or accurate.

There is still value for customers to read a professional review written by someone who does have the merit to write a considered review, or is a bona fide critic, rather than wading through pages of poorly written online reviews posted by previous customers with limited credibility. However, more and more potential customers favour reviews written from honest customer-like-me people who say it as they see it.

4.4 Events

Whereas a hotel has the ability to craft their reputation over time, events – which are temporary live happenings – do not have the luxury of longevity to develop a reputation, unless it is a regular repeat event such as an annual music festival.

For events, then, the external face of the event becomes critical in setting your promise to the customer. This is created through marketing collateral. The style of logo; the look and feel; the information; colours – each element suggests a perception of the event to the potential attendee so they know what to expect.

It used to be that when invitations were being sent by mail, a great deal of thought was put into the type of invitation – size of card; weight of paper; style of font; gold-edging – because the invitation was the first perception of the event which the customer would receive. It was the invitation which created customer expectation and set the tone of the event. The decision to attend an event would therefore rest on the quality of the invitation. That was a lot of responsibility for an invitation to carry, so it had to be carefully thought through.

Nowadays, the invitation does not carry such burden. This is not always a good thing because creating customer perception and expectation now entails a diverse range of marketing tools that need to be carefully planned, managed, and executed so that customer expectations at the event are met. Such tools include engagement with customers through social media, marketing campaigns, flyers, posters, and emails.

If the invitation is misaligned with creating the right customer expectation of the event, two things might happen. First, the purchasing decision whereby potential attendees may decide not to attend because the invitation fails to engage their interest or motivate them to spend their time and money to attend. A customer may even be in the situation of weighing the options to decide which event(s) to attend over this season, say.

Second, the customer satisfaction whereby customers will attend but their expectation (driven by the invitation) would not be met and there would be complaints, refunds, and damage to reputation.

Either way, the event would be unsuccessful due to the negative impact on revenue because not enough people attended, and damage to reputation by those who did attend but were disappointed with the experience they received.

AUTHOR'S VOICE

At a national stadium, I met the sales director and asked him what his target market is. He said "sales".

I was struck by his response because although he is a sales director, his job should not be to fill the stadium with any event that comes his way just because it represents a sale.

There are considerations for him other than sales or revenue, such as the reputation of his venue, ensuring events of good quality, having safe events, winning high-spend clients, winning high profile events that would enhance the profile of his venue, and winning international clients that attract international attendees.

If his targets were these kinds of events, it would generate better events with higher budgets. This, in turn, would attract further clients with better events and higher budgets. It wouldn't take very long for his stadium to build the profile and reputation for high-quality events rather than a venue that will take any booking just to gain a sale.

It is the difference between selling space and optimising the reputation of a flagship, landmark national event venue.

Winning events is all about reputation. A venue such as this should aim to win the best events with the highest budgets, not take anything it can get hold of.

There are textbooks on event planning and event marketing for further understanding of this topic, but what is key is the planning of marketing activities designed to engage customer interest in an event.

When planning the marketing of an event, thought must be given to the message, style, method, and honesty and not just to sell as many tickets as possible.

Customer perception, expectations, and setting customer expectations start from the outset of planning an event. It is that first invitation, email, or flyer which the customer sees that sets their expectations of the event. This first engagement with the customer sets the tone and is instrumental in engaging their interest when making the purchasing decision to participate with an event.

With events, the message can be corporate, professional, creative, fun, or appealing to a niche market. If the event is a conference, the message will be corporate and professional; if the event is a festival, party, or concert, the message will be creative and fun; if the event is a trade exhibition, the message will need to appeal to that niche market.

Events are experiential – they provide an experience to the customer. It is referred to as the *experience economy* defined as making money from providing experiences. This is what live events are for. Events provide a live experience which the customer could not get if they do not attend. Watching Glastonbury Festival on television, say, will not provide the same experience as being in the crowd in front of the Pyramid Stage at Worthy Farm in Somerset.

Even an event which is not for fun – a wake (celebration of life), perhaps – still needs to provide customers with a good experience. The food still has to be served hot, the staff still have to be welcoming and polite, the room still has to be cleaned and set up, and the service still needs to be efficient.

Providing experiences to customers requires engaging with their senses:

- **Sight** – what the event looks like and what is the visual content. This will involve decoration, flowers, lighting, the stage backdrop, screens and projection, lasers, special effects, and smoke machines. It includes the theme and concept of the event. And it includes the look and style of the venue to suit the type of event.

- **Hearing** – what the event sounds like such as type of music, style of music, quality of sound, sound levels, who is speaking, and what they say.

- **Taste** – what type of food will be served and what style of foodservice will it be. This extends to drinks, cocktails, and welcome canapés.

- **Smell** – what scents will the customer encounter such as smells of cooking or flowers. To fulfil this sense, event organisers utilise scent machines to fit the theme of an event such as woodland scents for a winter wonderland theme or scents of cinnamon, cloves, and orange for a Christmas party.

- **Touch** – what the customer will feel with the ambience of the event and will it be warm or cold, will they be engaging with physical activities to touch, and will they be carrying things away with them in physical form such as merchandise or a goodie bag.

AUTHOR'S VOICE

In the VIP lounge at the BRIT Awards, we filled the area with miniature rosemary trees. Beneath each tree were tealights that were lit to create a visual candlelight ambience. As the tealights warmed the rosemary trees, a fragrance of warm rosemary wafted through to welcome guests into the space.

The Manager must consider the sense-engaging elements of providing customers with an experience – an experiential event – and excite the customer through their sensory receptors.

AUTHOR'S VOICE

One problem I often encounter is the look of hotel banqueting suites. They are not appealing for the senses. Mostly, hotel banqueting suites are nondescript because they need to fit with a wide range of events from weddings to conferences. If the suite was decorated to suit weddings, it would not suit a business conference.

Some hotels of course do have exciting event facilities especially if it is a historic building with high ceilings and interesting architectural features. If not, it can take much time, effort, thought, creativity, and budget to transform a bland conference room into a fabulous event space.

Some of my event clients insist that I do not book their event into a hotel because they dislike that usual style of a banqueting suite, unless their event requires guests to stay overnight.

The problem for me when attempting to transform a banqueting suite is that they typically have low ceilings because hotel architects are governed by budget and it is cheaper not to build upwards.

Unfortunately, hotel architects fail to engage with event organisers to understand that we require high ceilings for lighting, projection, confetti canon, and other special effects needed to convert a boring space into an exciting venue and provide customers with a sensory experiential event.

Many hotels with bland event spaces and low ceilings will lose business because of the cost of decoration and the limits imposed by low ceilings. I wonder whether the costs saved during the build are merited by the loss of business throughout the life of the hotel.

For one thing, event organisers make money from providing creative elements at events. So, if there is no opportunity to import creatives, the organiser will find a venue where they can sell more to their client and up the budget.

This is why I always say, "the higher the ceiling, the higher the budget".

4.4.1 Setting Event Objectives

Every event has an objective. It starts with an idea – the reason to have an event in the first place. From there, it can be decided what are the objectives – what is the reason for this event; what does it need to achieve.

The purposes of objectives are these:

- To understand the reasons for the event and what it is intended to achieve
- To communicate to other stakeholders, the reasons for the event such as to clients, customers, sponsors, the press, suppliers, and staff
- To keep in focus the reasons for the event
- To track performance against objectives (during planning the event)
- To measure and evaluate performance against objectives (after the event)

An objective of an event can be to make a profit, or to give people a good time, or to raise funds for a charity. It might be to raise awareness of a new product – a product launch. Or it might be to bring people together to give them a message – a sales conference.

It is fine for more than one objective to be decided, so long as they support the success factors and do not conflict with each other. For example, a charity concert could have the objectives to raise funds for the charity, and to give customers a good time, and to raise awareness of the charity, and to achieve press coverage. In such cases, The Manager should identify the key objective but that is not always necessary because all objectives could be considered as being key.

AUTHOR'S VOICE

For me, safety is the priority objective. If an event is not safe, it cannot be a successful event. This is why, for me, every other objective falls beneath safety, and every element of the event has to be safe for it to achieve any other objective.

If I were to set customer satisfaction as the priority objective, and a customer gets injured because safety was a lower priority objective, it is not a successful event and would not have met the objective of customer satisfaction, anyhow.

INDUSTRY VOICE

"The events business is unique. The term 'event' is so diverse and can mean so many things to so many people.

It is important that every event is organised and delivered with a clear vision of what the aims and objectives are. How will success be measured and how do we achieve a product to be proud of.

With so many variations, one size does not fit all, but this should be celebrated across our industry".

James Young, Head of Events, Colchester Events Company

Once the event objectives are known, it is important to know whether they are on track to be met, and then if they were met. It would not make sense to set objectives and forget about them. Or not worry whether they are on track to be met. And not bother to conduct after-event evaluation to know whether the objectives were indeed met.

AUTHOR'S VOICE

My research reveals that most event organisers tend to focus on financial objectives. These are easier to measure than other objectives. For example, it is easier to measure the profit generated from an event or how many tickets were sold than to measure customer satisfaction. Financial objectives therefore take precedence over other key objectives such as client satisfaction, customer satisfaction, and safety.

Setting objectives is done before an event.

Keeping track of performance towards meeting the objectives is done during the planning phase, such as keeping track of how many tickets are selling.

Measuring objectives happens after an event has taken place, and it is easier to count the profit or count the tickets that were sold and how many entered through the front door. But it takes the after-event evaluation procedures outlined in 6.1 of this book to measure other objectives such as customer satisfaction.

Objectives need to be measured. This means an objective must be measurable. To say, "I want to make a profit from this event" is a wish rather than an objective. It is a loose, ambiguous statement and does not mean very much.

There needs to be a quantitative or statistical element for it to become an objective, such as "I aim to make £5,000 profit from this event" or "My objective is to make a profit of 20% of the total budget of this event". These are measurable and can be measured against during the planning of the event to know whether we are on track to make that £5,000 profit and measured post-event to know whether we did achieve that objective.

Quantifiable objectives allow for the identification of Key Performance Indicators (KPIs) to measure performance.

Let's say an objective for a charity event is to raise £5,000. That £5,000 target becomes the KPI to measure the performance against that objective. It will inform The Manager how the performance of ticket sales and sponsorships is contributing towards that target during the planning stage when tickets are being sold. After the event, The Manager will conduct accounting procedures and will measure against that KPI to see if the target of £5,000 was indeed met.

Not only do KPIs provide measures of performance to keep focus on the objectives and track the progress of performance against targets, they also help identify why targets were not achieved.

In the above example of raising £5,000 for a charity, but it was not met, the KPI measurement will help understand what impacted that objective. It could be that not enough tickets were sold, or the ticket price was too low, or the costs of the event were unexpectedly high so there was not enough left over to donate £5,000 to the charity.

But The Manager does not want to miss reaching the objectives. So, KPIs provide another function. If we keep with that example objective of £5,000 donated to a charity, other KPIs can be set to protect that objective and ensure it is met.

The costs of the event will be calculated into the budget. That cost calculation then becomes the KPI to measure the performance spend on costs. The number of tickets available to sell and the pricing points of tickets will be calculated so that the revenue generated from ticket sales is known and inserted into the budget. The ticket price also becomes a KPI and so does the number of tickets required to sell. Then, it can be tracked how ticket sales are performing. And it is known that ticket prices cannot be discounted because to do so would risk not meeting the KPI for ticket prices, and the objective to donate £5,000 to the charity would not be met.

Although objectives need to be quantifiable, they do not need to be financial. If the objective was to expose a new brand to customers attending an event, and that is the reason for the event to happen, it would be a wish. To quantify that objective would be to say that the brand will be exposed to 500 guests attending the launch party. The KPI would be the attendance of 500 guests. Responses to invitations would be monitored during the planning stage to know whether that target is on track. After the launch, the objective of exposing that brand to 500 guests would be measured against the KPI of actual attendees to know whether the objective was met.

Customer service is often high on the wish-list of event organisers because events are for people. But many event organisers will say that they want people to have a great time, which is the wish, and it gets left there. If you want people to have a good time at the event, customer satisfaction needs to be inserted as the objective, which means making customer satisfaction quantifiable; measurable.

A statistic which relates to customer satisfaction needs to be identified, such as 94% of customers are satisfied with the service at this event. Ninety-four per cent becomes the KPI. To measure this, a customer satisfaction survey will be carried out after the event to determine how many customers answered 'yes, I was satisfied with the service I received at this event'. The responses are measured against the KPI to know whether that event objective was met.

If a customer survey is not carried out after the event, The Manager will not determine that the event met its objective of satisfying customers because it was not measured. Okay, customers might have said it was fun when they left the event, but this is not measured or quantified; it is not constructive, it is not reliable, and it is subjective. *See 2.0 for measuring and monitoring customer satisfaction.*

Chapter 5

Contracts

In this chapter, we identify the merits of contracts in preventing litigation consequences and show why business should not be conducted without a contract in place. We outline the content of contracts and how they set expectations for all parties to prevent misinterpretations. Then we explain a simple but effective solution to prevent the problem of contracts not getting signed or getting delayed, and what to do if the supplier is not a professional or does not have a company.

5.0 Confirming the Promise with Contracts

A contract is a legally binding formal written agreement which details the expectations of what is being delivered against what has been requested.

Without a contract there is only a promise.

The problem is that promises can get broken by dishonest people, or because somebody over-promised and cannot deliver, or something is no longer possible to do, or something has changed such as the cost of an item making it no longer affordable, or it is no longer available, or somebody forgot to deliver what they said they would deliver, or because there was some mix-up or misinterpretation, etc. – That is a lot of risk of promises getting broken.

DOI: 10.4324/9781003154600-6

Promises are risky because even with good intentions there is risk of expectations not being delivered. The risk of a promise not being delivered is too great.

Broken promises are not only disruptive and inconvenient for The Manager or the staff but the impacts are felt by customers. If there is a let-down somewhere in the chain, the customer will experience that let-down. It might be that a menu item is not available because the supplier under-delivered what they promised. It could be that the DJ did not turn up for a party. If it occurs because of a broken promise, it will surely filter to the customer's experience of the service they receive.

Customer service levels will reduce if promises get broken – either promises from suppliers or promises to customers. For hotels, it is unacceptable for customer service levels to reduce. For events, a broken promise can jeopardise the entire event and there is no second chance to put it right.

There may be a verbal agreement but the content of a conversation is difficult to prove or argue and can be misinterpreted or incorrectly recalled to mind.

Emails can be vague, ambiguous, open to interpretation and misinterpretation, and may not be accepted in a court.

Businesses and customers of businesses cannot rely on promises alone. Promises need firming up into legally binding and obligated formal agreements: contracts.

When people are presented with a contract it changes from goodwill to a business transaction.

Requesting a contract or issuing a contract is an indication of professionalism and good business practice. Contracts protect people. It demonstrates that The Manager is not taking risks or relying on promises; they are concerned about doing things correctly, and they are intent on delivering. Nobody should want to do business without formal agreement of what is being promised.

A contract is not just a matter of dealing with mistrust. People may trust each other fully – they may have worked together repeatedly or be good friends – but if something were to go wrong through no fault or blame, it requires a contract to resolve arguments.

A contract is the planning for the potential of something going wrong.

A contract will pre-empt a situation in a proactive manner before a problem shows itself. So, a contract can help identify potential issues. Otherwise, it would be reactive problem solving after a situation has gone wrong. Writing or reading a contract focuses that person on what issues could arise and will help assess the probability of that issue arising and what impact it could have. It helps identify, assess, and mitigate the risks of something going wrong.

Things do go wrong for all manner of reasons which often cannot be predicted and may not be anybody's fault or blame.

If something does go wrong, it should be amicably resolved by dialogue. Talking brings people together. Silence and avoidance push people apart (see Chapter 7, *Dealing with Complaints*).

If it is not possible to talk, or talking has failed to resolve an issue, the contract comes into play.

The value of a contract becomes realised when things have not gone according to plan.

When writing a contract it should protect both parties from things going wrong and should be equally balanced so that it is fair and not loaded to benefit one party or another.

A contract must cover all elements that could possibly go wrong. But it has wider value than that.

A contract shows what has been requested and what is promised to deliver. It therefore provides expectations. It can include elements such as payment terms so that the customer understands what is expected of them and what obligations they are expected to meet. And it can include insurance details so there is no misinterpretation of who is expected to buy insurance.

If a wedding, say, confirms with a hotel, the contract will show how much it costs for the wedding to take place in that hotel and what is included within those costs:

Wedding on 25th May £10,000

- Included:
    - Hire of room 12:00 pm midday until 12:00 am midnight
    - Wedding breakfast menu B for 100 guests
    - 100 chairs
    - Ten round tables
    - White linen for ten tables

- Table glassware

- Ten waiting staff

- One microphone for speeches

- Dance floor

- Silver cake board and knife

- <u>Not included</u>:

  - Chair covers and sashes

  - Flower arrangements

  - DJ

  - Cake

  - Photographer

  - Evening buffet

The example above shows within the contract the expectations of what is included within the £10,000 cost of hiring the venue, and what is not included which would incur additional costs if the organiser decides to order them.

Some venues charge an all-inclusive package price which includes the hire fee and all other requirements. Other venues may charge a hire fee for use of the space only and then charge additionally for every item required. And some venues have some requirements included when the venue is hired but will charge for others, such as in the above example.

A venue will know what its pricing policy is, but an inexperienced event organiser such as a wedding client may not understand how venues charge in different ways.

The venue must make clear in the contract what is included and what is incurring additional charges to be open, transparent, and set the expectations.

A contract which sets out all the charges is not open to misinterpretation. This is important because some venues may have hidden charges, and other venues might show lesser charges to win the booking but then add further costs after the customer has booked.

A contract can also provide objectives which can be measured. For example, if a company were promoting a new product to an event audience at a festival, the statement within the contract might read like this:

"50 cases of new product for distribution to 500 guests attending the Berners & Martin Music Festival".

Here, the expectation is for the supplier to deliver 50 cases of the new product and the event organiser to distribute it to 500 guests attending the festival. The objective of that product reaching 500 attendees is measurable because it can be measured by how many attend the festival. If only 300 attend the festival, the objective would not be met and would breach the terms of the contract. The contract should stipulate what would happen in this situation. Either the surplus product would be returned to the supplier or could be retained for the next event, and this would be stated in the contract. It should also state who is counting the actual number of attendees at the event because this could potentially be a point of dispute.

It is usual for contracts to show an exchange.

In the wedding example above, the payment is £10,000 in *exchange* for use of the room between midday and midnight on 25th May, including the items listed.

In the Berners & Martin Music Festival example, 50 cases of product are provided in *exchange* for distributing it to 500 attendees at the festival.

As well as the exchange, a contract needs to show the following:

- The names and addresses of the parties

- The date

- Signatories

- Clauses

    Clauses can be cancellation terms, payment terms, late payment penalties, force majeure or acts of God, and insurances (see Berners, 2019 pp. 146–153).

It can be seen that the contract fulfils the following provisions:

- Provides expectations

- Provides objectives

- Provides legal obligations

- Provides clarity

- Provides an understanding of solutions if things were to go wrong

Contracts are a necessary tool to set out in writing the expectations of an agreement so there is no misinterpretation or ambiguity.

Being legally binding ensures both parties do in fact deliver their promises whether it is a venue providing services and resources, or a client providing the money for the booking. This way, contracts act to deter people from deviating the terms of the agreement. Without a contract, anybody might change their mind or let down the other party by not delivering on the promise.

It is essential to ensure that all exchanges are upheld by contracts whether it be with clients, suppliers and contractors, longstanding friends, reliable contacts, or somebody new.

AUTHOR'S VOICE

I work with suppliers with whom I have a long and trusted relationship; yet still I never ask for anything to be delivered without a contract. It is simply unprofessional to ask favours or promises. It leads to forgetfulness, let-downs, and disappointments.

I would think my suppliers now expect to be contracted by me and would find it odd if I didn't contract them.

I have had things go wrong during my career, such as complaints from clients or a supplier who lets me down, and it is the contract which gets me out of trouble. Either because it clarifies a point or because it details the route to find a solution.

The contract is one of the most valuable tools of my trade because it resolves dispute before it becomes too big to handle and would have to go to court.

If a client does not want to sign a contract, or they do not return it, or even if they delay the process there could be something wrong. Usually, it is because they have not reached a decision to go ahead with the booking. Sometimes, it requires somebody else in the organisation to approve and/or sign contracts such as the Chief Executive Officer (CEO) or Chief Finance Officer (CFO) and this can cause delay.

To prevent these delays, it is recommended not to accept a booking as confirmed until the contract is received signed by the client – and this would be stated in the contract. Every potential client should be made aware of this rule so that they understand from the outset that the date is not held for them and is not secure on the promise of a booking but is held provisionally pending receipt of the signed contract.

For a client to have made their choice of venue is a big step. Most times they would have spent much time and energy sourcing the most suitable venue and they would have had a lengthy process of identifying the right venue, visiting it for a show-round, discussing and negotiating with the venue manager, and receiving a proposal from the venue. By the time it comes to confirming the go-ahead for the event, the client needs that date held for them.

It is therefore a valuable incentive for the client to sign and return the contract to ensure that the venue is booked and the date is secured.

If a supplier does not want to sign a contract, it raises a red signal. All professional suppliers and contractors who are in business will be content and willing to sign a contract or present their contract to you.

For a contractor to work without a contract is a risk to them as well as to you – as stated previously, contracts protect both parties. If you find that a contractor or supplier is unwilling to be contracted, find another supplier.

If the supplier is not a professional or does not have a company – a friend of the bride who is supplying the wedding cake, say – there is still a need for contractual obligations. Just because it is an unprofessional transaction does not mean that the transaction cannot be professional!

You can set professional expectations and set these in writing to form the basics of a contract, such as type of cake; size of cake; what day and date it will be delivered; what time on that day it will be delivered; who will set it up, etc. Presenting these agreements in a formal document to the cakemaker will help to ensure that they treat their responsibilities in a professional manner and not as merely doing a favour to the bride.

Once a contract has been written, it can be used as the template for future clients and suppliers. This means that it is not an arduous task to raise a contract, each time. All it requires is an amendment of what is being delivered. In this fashion, a contract should be treated like a CV – the template is there as the foundation, but the details get tweaked to suit the job.

Most businesses – hotels, events, suppliers – will have a standard contract with the fundamental clauses in place which have been approved by a legal expert. These do not change.

To these, we can add amendments or 'schedules' to suit the job or the client. Some venues will have standard Schedule titles to add as additional pages such as Catering Schedule, Technical Schedule, and Other Requirements Schedule which are pre-formatted and populated, and completed to suit each booking.

Reference

Berners, P. (2019) *The Practical Guide to Managing Event Venues*. London: Routledge.

Chapter 6

Improving Customer Loyalty

In this chapter, we outline the need for repeat customers and how to retain them as continued loyal customers through the upward spiral of consistent customer service and ever-upward good experiences.

Section 6.1 details how leaders can drive customer loyalty by ensuring that their staff are in a happy state and will be effective in delivering high levels of customer service. This requires communication of the business goals through the hierarchical structure and we set out five tools for leaders to interact with their staff.

In Section 6.2, we visit customer loyalty at management level between leaders and staff. Here, it is identified how vital it is for communication to flow both downwards from leaders to staff and upwards from staff to leaders, using the management levels as the conduit. We look at how managers should behave in that 'middle' level.

Section 6.3 deals with customer loyalty at operational level with the staff and begins with effective communication. Here, we identify how staff who perform well are exposed to exploitation, and we take a look at how to deal with underperforming staff (Section 6.3.1) by focusing on their development into becoming good staff to support the objectives of the business.

Section 6.4 highlights communication as the essential component when dealing with staff who are delivering customer service. Here, we look at the Shannon &

DOI: 10.4324/9781003154600-7

Weaver model which demonstrates how messages can be interrupted by 'noise' and why obtaining feedback is necessary. We guide you through the process of effective communication (Section 6.4.1) using the 7Cs model by Cutlip & Center. We then journey through hotel interdepartmental communication (Section 6.4.2) and consistency of performance (Section 6.4.3), event interdepartmental communication (Section 6.4.4), and event processes of communication (Sections 6.4.5–6.4.7) before arriving at departmental communication (Section 6.4.8).

6.0 Repeat Customers

The objective of any business is to satisfy customers. Having happy customers is confirmation that The Manager is doing a great job.

It is more than that, though. If customers are happy they will stay longer and spend more money, and they will return to spend even more money. Happy customers = profit.

If customers feel happy with the service they have received at an event or in a hotel, they will return to repeat that enjoyable experience. It takes time and effort for customers to find new places they like and enjoy. It is safer to return to a place they already know they like. It lessens the risk of landing in a place they do not like and may have to complain.

Luckily for event and hotel businesses, customers are habitual and social creatures. They enjoy returning to the same social places. It creates familiarity, memories, associations, and friendships.

Often, of course, customers who are familiar with a hotel or event and know they will receive good service will bring their social network – friends and family. If they are wanting to have a good time in a social setting, they will want to do so with people they know. They will mostly do this at places they know because they want a guarantee to show their friends or family. After all, it is their judgement at stake. If they are known to the staff, organiser, or hotelier, it taps deeper into their social needs and they will feel very good about that.

Happy customers become loyal customers.

Repeat customers are essential because it brings business in without requiring the effort and costs of reaching new customers through marketing initiatives and then having to win them over. Repeat customers are already won over which is why they have returned, and it costs nothing to get them back into the business to spend more of their money. But, now we need to retain them as loyal customers, so we must continue to provide consistent customer service and ever-upward good experiences.

More and more events are becoming regular fixtures to capitalise on customer loyalty by generating a longer-term reputation. Event organisers are looking to create loyal customers who are already won over and will eagerly await tickets to go on sale for the next event. An event can sell out to repeat attendees. Or at least a good proportion of tickets will be sold to repeat customers before needing to spend on marketing to attract and engage new attendees. It does require previous events to satisfy customers; otherwise, they will not return, and the reputation of the event will be damaged. So, The Manager has to be especially careful to set customer expectations, manage customer expectations, and deliver good customer service. It also requires The Manager to assess whether the customers are satisfied after each previous event so they can learn and improve the next event. Event assessment is achieved by conducting the after-event procedures of feedback and evaluation (see 2.0).

AUTHOR'S VOICE

I was briefly working with a hospice which is a very valuable service to society. Their fundraising team were running events to support the considerable costs of the hospice. The success of these events was essential.

But the organisers of the events in the fundraising team were not trained or educated in running events so they did not understand the value of feedback and evaluation to ensure participants were happy and to learn what could be improved and developed. So, a lot of the events the hospice organised were short-lived and tended to fizzle out.

One event manager told me that they were stopping a particularly large event because it had reached its optimum. I asked her how she knew that – had she conducted a participant survey; had she explored growth opportunities; had she consulted with people who could suggest growth and development strategies for that event; had she set objectives which had been reached or were yet to be reached?

She answered that the event had run its course, people were bored with it, and it had stopped making money so it was time to drop it from the annual calendar of events.

She may have been right. But she couldn't know she was right because she hadn't done the evaluation. Because of that, there might have been further opportunities for that event to continue contributing funds to the hospice which needs every help it can get – which, after all, is the job the fundraising team are getting paid for.

Further to this, however, is the need to continue the upward spiral of delivering better, more creative and higher experiential events so as to retain attendees into the future. Again, feedback and evaluation are important here to ascertain what could be improved, what customers would like to see next time, and what would keep them returning.

Selling tickets to returning customers allows for the growth of an event because there will be a loyal customer base plus new customers to attract. If there are no returning customers or too few, new customers will need to be attracted each year, and the event will struggle to grow.

If there is going to be a repeat event in the future – next year, say – the objective of the current event should be to sell a proportion of tickets for that future event. Remember, the objective needs to be quantifiable so The Manager will need to set a target number of tickets to be sold at the current event for the next event. This will be measurable, and The Manager will understand whether the objective is on track (see Section 4.4.1). There are mechanics to facilitate this objective. The Manager might offer incentives such as discounted ticket prices to current customers if they buy a ticket now for the future event. This creates the current event as a 'leader' event to generate sales for forthcoming events.

What The Manager is trying to do is guarantee sales for the future event and get money in the bank to begin spending on the future event such as securing the venue and booking the performers. It is not too soon to sell tickets for an event next year because the point is to capture those already enjoying the event this year.

AUTHOR'S VOICE

I joined a company that organised an annual golf tournament on the Algarve for top leaders in the pub industry.

There were limited tickets, and it was a valuable networking opportunity for these key industry leaders.

It was a successful event each year, but every year the organiser would finish the event and leave it alone for ten months until it rolled around again in the calendar. Then she would dust it off and begin marketing the event to sell tickets, but it was always a struggle to engage key people and sign them up to attend.

I suggested selling tickets at the current golf event for next year's tournament to capitalise on the loyalty of the people who were with us enjoying their golf experience. It was a captured market. It worked. It was easy to lengthen the participants' experience by selling tickets for next year's event, and it created a 'see you next year' camaraderie among the golfers.

Why wait to begin marketing a cold event from scratch when you've already got a hot one happening?

It meant we could secure the venue a year in advance at a good price and we could continue our engagement with confirmed customers during the countdown to the next event.

We could also relax in the knowledge that the event was sold out which allowed us to switch focus on other events in our portfolio.

Loyal customers will tell other potential customers and do the marketing job free of charge by word of mouth. People create the reputation (they can damage it, too) so if the event or hotel is delivering great service above customer expectations, the happy customers are instrumental in the success of the business. It is an upward spiral (Figure 6.1).

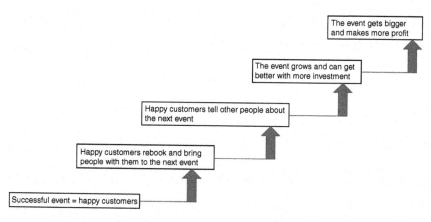

Figure 6.1 Upward Spiral of Success

6.1 At Leadership Level

Driving customer loyalty upward at leadership level begins with one thing: happy staff.

Leadership is about people. It is the responsibility of leaders to ensure that the people in their team at an event or hotel are delivering excellent customer service which is difficult for staff to do if they are dissatisfied, disgruntled, or unhappy.

It is possible, however, to achieve a level of customer satisfaction with staff who are not very happy because some staff members will be good with customers even if they are unhappy themselves. A proportion of the staff will be professional in their service, or they may be trained, or they just might have the personal attributes to perform their job well and keep their customers happy.

But those team members who are good with customers is a proportion of the team and we are not looking for proportional customer satisfaction. We want total customer satisfaction which requires all our staff to be happy.

Besides, if the team as a whole are unhappy, even those good ones will eventually tire of carrying the burden and they will become unhappy themselves or will leave.

It will certainly be harder for an event or hotel to provide customer satisfaction if the team is unhappy, and it will not be at the highest possible level.

Some staff will need the job whether they are happy at work or not, so it is a form of exploitation for The Manager to demand good customer service from a team who are not happy to do so.

Customers want to be served by genuinely happy staff if they are going to support the business with their custom. If they are choosing to spend their money at that event or hotel, they are participants, and no customer wishes to participate in a business that cannot make their staff happy to be working there.

Everybody wants to work in a friendly and likeable socio-professional environment where they feel enjoyment. With the additional benefit of driving customer satisfaction upward, leaders must focus on ensuring that staff are happy.

Leaders of a business cannot expect their customers to be happy if the staff serving them are unhappy.

At leadership level in a hierarchical socio-professional structure, the focus should be on good communication with the next level down which might be managers, heads of department, or supervisors. For events, it could be assistant managers, department managers, or technical managers. Let's call them 'middle managers'.

Middle managers hold the power to convey messages from leadership to the staff and communicate staff issues to the leaders. Hierarchical management has worked well over many years if the communication is well structured. However, contemporary management models favour flatter structures with less formal lines of communication.

Whatever the hierarchical structure, it is important that the workforce pull together to achieve the goals of the business. This requires an understanding of what the business goals are. Leaders will know the goals, of course. Middle managers will probably know the goals or some of the goals. But staff do their job often with their own objectives in mind (such as getting paid) which may not be in alignment with the business goals or they might not understand what the business goals are. For one thing, the goal for a business is to make money, whereas the goal for a member of staff is to take money from the business. It is an exchange, of course – the business cannot make money from serving customers if there are no staff, and the business will take more money from customers than it gives to its staff, but it is a misaligned objective, nonetheless.

If staff are integral in achieving the goals of the business, such as delivering excellent customer service, consistent customer service, maintaining high standards, achieving customer satisfaction, encouraging customer retention, repeat customers, achieving new customers, driving sales upward, achieving profit targets, etc., then they need an understanding what these goals are and their role in achieving them for the success of the business. Staff also need to understand where there are successes and failures.

Leaders are typically distanced from staff which is why middle managers become important because they bridge that distance.

Leaders may not undertake speaking to every member of staff, every day, to ensure that they are aligned with the business goals, which is why they must communicate the goals to middle managers who work alongside their staff. This is the point of middle managers. There would be no requirement for them if leaders worked closely with staff, but this is not possible when leaders are not 'on the floor'. The answer is for leaders to communicate with the fewer middle managers, and the middle managers to convey the messages to their staff.

Just because it is impracticable for leaders to interact with all staff every day, does not absolve them of the responsibility to ensure staff within their organisation are happy.

This is important because we have already identified how happy staff are crucial in driving customer satisfaction upward.

It is still possible, and necessary, for leaders to interact with staff by using the following tools:

> **AUTHOR'S VOICE**
>
> Leaders should not treat their staff as 'staff'.
>
> 'Staff' are made up of individual people and they should be treated and acknowledged as individuals.
>
> As a venue manager, I would speak to each member of my staff as an individual. This means I would treat each person differently at each time I met them.
>
> So, if I was saying hello to Jack, I would talk to him as Jack, not as a staff member. And whenever I was with Jack, I would talk to him according to the situation we were meeting. If it was in the lunchroom, I would be relaxed and friendly with Jack. If it was during an event, I would be more formal and instructive. If it was for a disciplinary, I would be further distant but focused on correcting his behaviour.
>
> Each time, I adjusted my interaction with the person I was speaking with and in what situation I was engaging with them. That, for me, is leadership.

- **Appraisals**

  Leaders should conduct staff appraisals as a structured and planned method of interacting with staff to acknowledge their achievements, identify any issues, discuss working conditions, identify training needs, decide progression and development plans, and learn if staff are happy or find resolutions to keep them happy.

  Often, the job of conducting staff appraisals is delegated to line managers because they work alongside the staff members. But because they work together, a line manager is already informed about the performance of their staff and they have a relationship with them. Staff appraisals, therefore, provide the opportunity for a leader to engage with the staff and learn what is going on in their organisation. A leader should want to conduct staff appraisals for this reason. To be informed and prepared, the leader should meet with the line manager before the staff appraisal happens.

- **Rewards and incentives**

  Staff are motivated by recognition of their good standards and achievements or for achieving results aligned with the business goals. If the reward or incentive is awarded by a leader, it carries more gravitas.

- **Regular meetings**

  A leader should hold regular structured meetings with staff to uphold good levels of communication. Typically, leaders hold Management Meetings, Operations Meetings, and Heads of Department meetings. They should also conduct meetings which include staff such as 'staff voice' meetings or monthly 'all staff' meetings.

- **Open-door policy**

  The hierarchical structure may include middle managers, but this should not prevent staff from being able to meet with a leader. Leaders should ensure that there is a process where staff have the opportunity to request a meeting with a leader.

- **Anonymous feedback**

  If there is an open-door policy for staff to meet a leader, they may not wish to do so because of nervousness, sensitivities, or there is a situation involving their manager or another colleague. Providing the opportunity to submit anonymous feedback to a leader encourages staff to be open about any issues they are dealing with and is another valuable tool in ensuring staff are happy.

I would ask a leader, "Are your staff happy? How do you know?"

6.2 At Management Level

Managers are positioned in the middle between leaders and staff. These middle managers are responsible for communicating from leaders to staff, and staff to leaders. Often, middle managers are adept at the former but not the latter. There is an assumption that communication flows just one way – downwards, like a waterfall. Yet, if managers are positioned in the middle, it should be a balanced role and communication should equally flow upwards, too.

Leaders tend to send messages down the hierarchy and feel their job is done. But a leader should relish receiving communication from the lower ranks and encourage two-way communication through the hierarchy via the conduit of their managers. Managers must position themselves to communicate upwards to the leader as the counterbalance for passing the leader's messages downwards to the staff.

Generally, there is acceptance that managers deal with staff problems and issues and do not bother the leader with such low-level operational issues. This approach is counterproductive to the goals of the business which rest on the happiness of staff – we have already identified that happy staff are integral to achieving happy customers (customer satisfaction) = higher sales and greater profit.

By having managers in place, a leader is one-step removed from the staff so it becomes important for The Manager to bring the leader closer to what is happening at staff-level so that the goals of the business are truly and fully aligned from top to bottom and back up again. It is the way to identify if there are problems occurring which threaten the business objectives so that corrective steps can be taken.

Leaders should want to know what is happening at staff-level, and it is The Manager's responsibility to communicate it to them. Unfortunately, many leaders are not really interested to know what is happening at staff-level, which is simply poor leadership. That makes The Manager's job more difficult but should not prevent them from doing it.

Managers require a good and trustful working relationship with their staff (and their leader). Managers can struggle with this concept because it can be difficult for a manager to distinguish the narrow line of professionalism from friendliness. Managers want to be friendly with their staff but are in a higher level in the hierarchy and need to maintain discipline and distance. This balance of distance and friendliness is often a conundrum for managers.

The solution is to be a friendly manager without being friends with the staff. It is not easy and requires time to develop the professional characteristics of being friendly but not a friend.

The key – and it is a complex one – is in understanding that each member of staff is different and every situation is different. This means each encounter, with each member of staff, each time, is individual and The Manager's approach needs to adjust with each. This makes that line between friendly and friend a jagged haphazard zigzag (which is the difficulty) because a manager needs to constantly adjust their behaviour to each staff member in each situation they encounter.

Performed adeptly, this jerky waltz allows The Manager to draw close and withdraw; in and out; close and distant; rise and fall without being either too close or too distant.

Over time, staff will identify the steps which keeps their manager friendly but not a friend (not too close) and professional (not too distant) and will not be able to rely on set precedents such as over-familiarity or favouritism, or even dislike.

By performing as described above, managers will find it possible to be friendly but professional with their staff which is essential for trustful engagement, openness, and free but trustful communication. This is helpful with their role in communicating a range of messages from a leader and conveying issues from staff to a leader.

Managers are not in place to prevent or obstruct communication. They are there to facilitate communication.

6.3 At Operational Level

Staff want to be happy. They are desperate for it. Nobody wants to go to work and have a miserable day.

The social merits of working are well-documented and are visible with mental well-being because human beings are social beings. Lockdowns and working from home evidenced the need for social interaction, and most people were extremely happy to return to the office social environment.

Staff are motivated by knowing they are doing a good job and getting paid for having done so. Knowing they are doing a good job is reflected by praise and recognition from leaders, managers, and customers.

Motivated and happy staff are delighted to continue to deliver good customer service – they relish doing so because that is the value and reward of their job. It is why staff show it on their CV with statements such as *I like working with people; I'm good with people; I'm a good team-player.*

It is important to reflect the achievements of staff by giving praise and recognition.

There are no benefits to having unhappy staff.

Now we know this, what are the causes of staff being unhappy?

Usually, it is poor communication. Poor communication leads to miscommunication, misinterpretation, and misunderstanding.

Staff want to know what is happening and they want to understand how it affects them. They also want to be heard.

Hearing your staff is essential for their happiness; otherwise, their problems will grow to unhappiness.

Often, their problems seem mundane and trivial but if it matters to them as a person, it should matter to you.

Instead of considering staff issues as trivial, consider that the more trivial they are, the easier they are to fix!

AUTHOR'S VOICE

I quite enjoy talking with my staff about their problems. It provides a social opportunity and we are all social beings. The real benefit, how-ever, is that I would rather my staff tell me if they are unhappy about something, than go and tell somebody else.

A frequent unhappiness for staff is being given responsibilities above the job they are being paid to do. This makes people unhappy first because they are not being paid to undertake those responsibilities, but also because if those responsibilities are higher, that is not the position they are in or have chosen.

This is a frequently occurring problem which makes staff less happy when their job role grows to take on more responsibility, but their job title and pay remain as they were. This can happen with competent and motivated staff who accept or get given more responsibilities because they are good at the job. In a way it is lazy management to apportion more responsibility to staff who happen to be competent. It is also unfair to increase a job role without increasing the pay.

It raises an ethical issue too because the staff member wants to keep their job and not upset their manager, so they are manipulated into accepting more re-sponsibilities for the same reward which is exploitation. It is trying to get the most work from someone for the least cost.

This practice has the effect to penalise good staff for doing a good job by dumping more responsibility into their role. Good performance deserves reward through pay, promotion, or development.

This type of practice does not help with the motivation and happiness of staff in the goal to drive customer satisfaction upward. Over time, staff will realise that they are being exploited for doing a good job and will either learn to underper-form or harbour feelings that their goodwill is being abused.

Eventually, those exploited staff will leave for a job where they get rewarded for those additional responsibilities – that is, promotion. If a member of staff has grown to accept more responsibility because they have proved they are compe-tent and good at their job, they are ripe to receive promotion. So, if they are not going to be promoted in the job they are in, they will move to an employer who is offering a higher job. It is called career progression.

The best approach with staff is for The Manager to reflect how they would feel if they were being asked to do something. This is the value of a manager having risen through the ranks and knowing how to do the job they are asking their staff to perform. Reflecting upon your experiences at that time – and how they made you feel and perform your job – will help you understand the feelings of your staff.

6.3.1 Underperforming Staff

If a member of staff is underperforming, the first priority is to understand why. To understand why, requires questions.

The rule with a member of staff who is not performing well is to sit with them and ask questions.

Whatever their answers, knowing the problem allows The Manager to find solutions or make reasonable adjustments. It could be a change in work pattern, further training, a transfer to another role or department.

AUTHOR'S VOICE

I had a member of staff who always arrived late. I didn't mind because there were other staff who could cover his lateness.

His lateness became a habit which became an expectation and I came to accept it. That was my mistake. I was unfairly expecting other members of the team to routinely perform another person's duties. This was poor management. I was also ignoring the issue. I was showing him that I didn't even care why he was always late. And I was showing the team that I didn't care they were covering for him.

On top of this, the team was fragmenting because one of them was always late and the others were frustrated at having to cover for their late colleague, and their manager wasn't interested in doing anything about it.

In truth, I only acted when it became necessary, which was already too late.

I sat down with the late guy and by asking questions, I learnt that he was caring for a family member at home and had to wait until somebody took over before he could leave the house and come to work. He hadn't informed me because he didn't want to use it as an excuse and thought he was coping well.

His work was his escape and relief from being a carer, so this job mattered to him. If I hadn't sat with him but fired him for his lateness, I would have put him in a very serious situation socially, psychologically, and financially.

I also learnt that if he didn't leave the house on time, he would miss his train and have to wait for the next one which made him late.

Knowing this information, I rostered him to begin at a later time and rearranged the other staff rosters to ensure that there were adequate staff on duty, and they weren't 'covering' him. Because I gave him a generously later start time, he was always early because of the train schedule, and it wasn't long before he was helping the team with their duties even though he wasn't yet rostered to begin his shift. The change in attitude of the team was visible, and as a leader, I felt good about finding a workable resolution.

It is lazy management to ignore the issue and simply accept that one member of staff is not as good as other members of the team. The Manager should allow good staff to get on with the job and focus their attention to helping underperformers become good staff.

AUTHOR'S VOICE

I find that a lot of managers focus on good workers in their team. They like good staff and so they become the favourites. They give them rewards, the better jobs, and the better shifts.

I do the opposite. I focus my attention on any member of my team who is underperforming. I treat it as a project to find out why, find solutions, and turn that person's performance around. I challenge myself to improve their performance, and if they do, that is the reward for me, my staff, and my business.

So, I let the good staff get on with their job because I can trust they will do so. And I turn my attention to the underperformer. Doesn't it make sense to improve the performance of underperformers rather than spend time with those who are already performing well?

Staff are not The Managers or leaders in an organisation which means they seek good leadership. They want good communication and an understanding of the goals of the business. And they want a friendly and professional manager: someone who engages with them and listens to them, is supportive, trustful, and honest, but is not over-familiar nor too distant.

If leaders and managers deliver what staff want, their staff will be happy.

6.4 The Communication Process

Communication is the component which threads through everything in this book and everything about good service, achieving goals, and keeping staff happy. It is often considered that for every problem encountered, trace it back to source and you will find it arrived from poor communication. Try that!

Communication is the act of sending a message from its source (the sender) to its destination (the receiver). A problem often occurs in how the message gets transmitted from the sender to the receiver. During the process of that message travelling from its source to its destination, there is risk of 'noise' which interrupts the flow or meaning of the message. This can be seen in the Shannon & Weaver Model of Communication shown in Figure 6.2.

The Shannon & Weaver model shows the linear flow of a message being sent from its source through a transmitter (such as a phone line), via a channel of communication (the telephone), to a place where it is decoded (the message is interpreted by the person answering the phone) and is received at its destination.

The potential for miscommunication is at the point of the channel, which is the method chosen to send the message. Here, there is potential for 'noise' to disrupt or interrupt the message being successfully received.

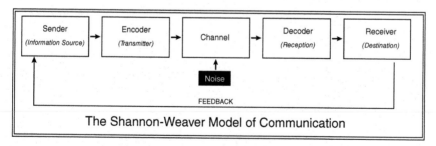

Figure 6.2 The Shannon & Weaver Model of Communication

'Noise' is not necessarily loud or even audible – it refers to anything that could interfere with the message. In the case of a phone call, it could be actual noise such as distortion or background noise but it could also be 'noise' caused by a break in the signal which ceases the call or even that there was no answer at the receiver's end. In each case, the message was interrupted or disrupted, which is referred to as 'noise'.

Let's ensure that this point is understood because if the message is channelled as an email, there would not be any actual noise. The 'noise' could be that the email was not received, or it bounced back, or it was not read in time, or it went to the junk folder – these are interruptions or disruptions of the message being successfully transmitted from source to destination: 'noise'.

Even when the message is transmitted from person to person, it can be interrupted or disrupted by noise. It could be an audible noise and the hearer cannot hear what the speaker is speaking but it could also be a simple misinterpretation of an instruction and that would also be 'noise'.

Look again at that model in Figure 6.3. Notice the narrow black line returning from the receiver to the sender. This line represents feedback which is important because it demonstrates that the receiver of the message must provide feedback to the sender, which means that the sender must ask the receiver for feedback.

Feedback can be a simple confirmation that the message was received. If it is channelled verbally by telephone or in person, feedback can be the question, 'Do you understand what I need you to do?' or better still, 'Can you confirm what I need you to do'. By email, the sender can end the message with, 'Please confirm when you have read this message' or 'Please let me know when you have done what I've asked'.

In short, feedback is the check. It checks that the message was received, but most importantly, it was understood; that it was interpreted correctly; that it was received in time for an action to happen; that it was received by the correct receiver; that it is possible to do. Feedback checks there was no 'noise'.

Feedback checks whether there are any questions, or is there a need for a piece of equipment, say. If the message is 'Please provide Mr Berners with a generous discount', the check might be how much discount, or do you have a key to override the till to provide the discount.

This model helps The Manager understand the process of communication, the presence of the risk of noise which can interrupt or disrupt the message, and the need to request feedback to check the message was received and interpreted correctly by the person it was intended to reach.

The 7 Cs of Effective Communication

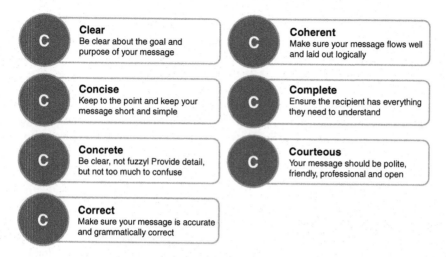

Clear
Be clear about the goal and purpose of your message

Coherent
Make sure your message flows well and laid out logically

Concise
Keep to the point and keep your message short and simple

Complete
Ensure the recipient has everything they need to understand

Concrete
Be clear, not fuzzyl Provide detail, but not too much to confuse

Courteous
Your message should be polite, friendly, professional and open

Correct
Make sure your message is accurate and grammatically correct

Figure 6.3 Cutlip & Center's 7 Cs of Effective Communication

6.4.1 Effective Communication

People communicate all the time. But how much of what they communicate is effectively communicated?

Figure 6.3 shows a model by Cutlip and Center (Broom and Bey-Ling, 2013) which demonstrates the seven components required for communication to be effective.

According to this model, there are 7 Cs required for communication to be effective. When we communicate, how many of us include all these 7 Cs? There are people who do not communicate Courteously because they are busy or stressed. Sometimes, the message being communicated is not Correct, or it is not Complete. We all know people who start a conversation midway and we have to ask them to start at the beginning – to be Complete.

Some people waffle and are told to get to the point – be Concise.

The issue is that if one of the 7 Cs is missing, the communication is not effective.

The 7 Cs of effective communication is easy to read on paper, just like most theoretical models of management. The problem is they are not easy to remember in practice – when they are needed to be enacted. Who walks around doing their job with a piece of paper to remind them of management models such as the 7 Cs of effective communication – that you need to say this Clearly, Concisely, Concretely, Correctly, Coherently, Completely, and Courteously?

It is less easy still to apply theoretical models of management in the job. They get forgotten, they are too complex, and there is no time during an event or busy shift to consider the 7 Cs and work out how to implement them.

The point of theoretical models is not so much to implement but to educate. Such models inform The Manager and become part of their makeup as a good leader – and in the case of the 7 Cs, an effective communicator. If The Manager has awareness and understanding of theoretical applications, it becomes part of who they are, so when it comes to doing the job, it is not necessary to think about applying a model because it has been considered in the approach or the planning.

AUTHOR'S VOICE

I don't consciously think about applying models of management. I don't sit and consider them. But, because I am informed about them, it means they fit somewhere within the makeup of me doing my job.

For example, I might be planning a pre-event production meeting or an onsite staff briefing and I will be aware of how to communicate effectively, which I couldn't do if I didn't know about it. I could refer to the 7 Cs model now that I am informed and aware of it, and I feel sure that would be helpful when I am writing my briefing notes, but in the real world of being busy and distracted, it is enough to be informed and aware so that I can at least apply some part of it and be more effective if not fully effective.

The Shannon & Weaver Model of Communication isn't at the forefront of my mind every time I send an email. But I am aware of what it means – noise can disrupt the message – so I will consider how best to convey that message and who is receiving it. And I do now always ask for their feedback to check it was received and interpreted correctly.

These models are learning – education – and with all learning, education, and experience, it develops the way we do our job.

Education provides The Manager with an armoury of knowledge and understanding. Theoretical models supply that armoury – they are in the toolbox to reflect upon, consider, and refer to if something did not work out the right way, or when planning and preparing future actions.

It does not take a great deal of time to consider the Shannon & Weaver model and think about what 'noise' could interrupt a message being sent from the sender to the receiver and consider how that risk can be mitigated. Knowing this model and the impact of noise when communicating messages is how education informs The Manager in the job because not knowing means it will not be considered and the risk of miscommunication is greater.

6.4.2 Hotel Interdepartmental Communication

Hotels by nature are split into departments and become departmentalised. Often, staff in one department have little or no interaction with staff in another department and an accepted socio-structural culture develops where staff working in one department become alienated from staff in other departments.

When this happens, staff in one department have little knowledge of how interrelated departments work and the impacts one department has on another. Reception has a direct interrelation with housekeeping for instance. The banqueting department has direct interrelation with kitchen. Not all interrelationships are easily identifiable or appreciated, however.

The Manager should make attempts to avoid departmentalisation becoming a problem. Some hotels implement regular social occasions for staff to mix, build cross-department relations, and encourage interdepartmental communication and appreciation. Some hotels have an induction scheme where new recruits work in all departments to gain knowledge of other departments and meet staff and managers outside their own regular department. Other hotels may have a graduate training scheme for students entering the industry who benefit from training and experience in all departments of a hotel.

Inter-department social events, induction programmes across departments, and graduate training schemes are attempts to improve channels of communication across departments of the hotel so there becomes an appreciation of how other departments work and the impacts one department has upon another. An additional benefit is the cross-training of staff who can be deployed across the hotel where business levels demand. This supports customer satisfaction by limiting gaps in service. An example might be where the bar becomes suddenly busy, and by having the ability to bring bar-trained waiters from the restaurant or a bar-trained receptionist from front office fills the gap in service and restores customer satisfaction at the bar.

In achieving the goal of complete customer satisfaction, it is important that all staff understand that theirs is not the only department or the most important department, but all departments of the hotel interact fluently and efficiently in supporting the goals of the business.

AUTHOR'S VOICE

The Edge Hotel School at the University of Essex has a fully commercial four-star country house hotel on campus where students studying hospitality management, hotel management, and events management gain live practical experience alongside academic study, lectures, assessments, and exams.

In the hotel, students in their first year perform operational staff duties under the supervision of second-year students. In their second year, it is their turn to supervise first-year students. And when they move to their third year, they take on management roles such as duty management and night management.

Throughout their journey of education, each student 'rotates' through every department of the hotel to gain an understanding of the different roles of each department but also how they are affected by good (or poor) interdepartmental communication and the impacts each department has on the running of the hotel in achieving the goals of the business.

The 'rotation' system enables students working as staff to cross-train and be ready to work in any department of the hotel and it gives them confidence and practical skills for when they enter the industry.

The Manager should be careful not to force or pressure a member of staff to work in another department. Remember, each staff member is an individual person and cannot all be treated the same way. There may be reasons why somebody does not want to work in a certain other department, but anyway, they did not choose that other department to work in.

You can encourage cross-training and highlight the benefits to the education, skillset, and knowledge of the staff member as well as the benefits to the business, but it should not be mandatory for a housekeeper to work in the kitchen, say.

6.4.3 Hotel Interdepartmental Consistency of Performance

Because hotels are departmentalised, there can be variances in performance from one department to another. This is not helpful for customer satisfaction because the customer experience will be inconsistent on their journey through your hotel.

AUTHOR'S VOICE

I was working as the Head of Events for a corporation for just over a year before they decided we should all work in another department. Mine was to go out on newspaper delivery vans all night.

Well, as an event organiser, I don't mind working all night long, but I could not see the benefits of me spending a night delivering newspapers. I'd been in the job a year already so it didn't seem a necessary requirement for my performance. Also, I had been recruited because of my career history and ability to do the job, so why would I now need to go out on the nightly delivery vans?

I declined to participate in the initiative. But, if I had been forced to put myself through what I could only see as a pointless exercise, it would have placed me in a mindset completely against what the initiative had been set up to achieve!

The customer might go to the bar and enjoy that experience, but when they move through to the restaurant, they could receive a less-enjoyable experience.

Departments in a hotel need to perform a waltz – the moving-together at the same tempo and rising and falling in unison. Jerky movements are not welcome in providing consistent customer service.

The Manager should establish departmental benchmarks to measure the performance of one department against another. So, a benchmark for the bar could be the low level of staff turnover because the bar staff are treated well and are happy. That low level of staff turnover becomes the benchmark for the other departments. It can then be identified which departments are underperforming against that benchmark if their staff turnover level is higher. The department with the highest gap from the benchmark requires some attention to identify why staff are unhappy and are leaving and what lessons can be learnt from the bar department in the way they retain their staff.

Interdepartmental benchmarking can be implemented for every measurable key performance indicator. Staff turnover is an obvious one, but there are others such as profit margins achieved per department; departmental costs as a percentage of their profit; spend per head from customers across departments; customer satisfaction levels and customer comments from surveys, feedback and comment cards that relate to the service they receive from each department; and levels of repeat bookings and returning customers achieved by departments.

INDUSTRY VOICE

"One of the key factors affecting consistency in the hospitality industry is employee turnover. It is ineffective and inefficient to continually re-cruit and train new team members, let alone maximise the performance of existing team members. As a result, not enough time is spent on quality people development and quality management practices.

By creating the best possible employee experience and the right envi-ronment for people to excel, we can retain and develop talent to deliver the highest standards on a consistent basis".

Adam Rowledge, Managing Director, Rowledge Associates

6.4.4 Event Interdepartmental Communication

Events are less structured and departmentalised than hotels. And because they are typically short-term one-off events, they do not suffer the long-term accepted socio-habits which evolve over time and become embedded in the culture of a fixed business.

Even so, events are comprised of a range of specialists who come together to produce an event. These include the event management team; the venue; pro-duction (staging, technical crew); security; catering; and theme and decoration. For complex events, it could extend to sponsorship; accounting; entertainment; transport; accommodation; safety; medical; VIP handling; press handling; public relations; and marketing.

Although event hierarchy and departmentalisation differ from hotels, there is need for effective interdepartmental communication across events so that each area is working towards the success of the event.

Unlike the static structure of hotels, an event team comes together for the one-time project. It is important, therefore, to identify and communicate the objec-tives of the event to the project team. This cannot be taken for granted because not all events have the same objectives. Every event will want to provide attend-ees with a good experience, but there are other objectives for an event to be successful (see Section 4.4.1).

The objectives of an event need to be understood by key managers and commu-nicated to all levels of staff involved with contributing to the success of the event. To achieve this requires project or production meetings, pre-event briefings, and onsite staff briefings.

- **Project or Production Meetings**

Production meetings are held at regular intervals during the pre-event planning phase called the 'lead-in'. The lead-in is the time between confirmation that the event is going ahead (it is contracted) and the date of the event.

During the lead-in, The Manager will schedule a series of production meetings with key team members to co-ordinate communication and ensure that the event objectives are communicated and on track to be achieved. Usually, it begins with monthly production meetings which become more frequent as the lead-in shortens, so they might occur weekly as the event nears. This largely depends on the complexity of the event.

- **Pre-event Briefings**

In the days leading up to the event date, The Manager will hold a pre-event briefing with key team members and other team members to bring the entire team together. At this meeting, the team will communicate strategies, key information, and objectives.

Often, the pre-event briefing is for staff if it is not appropriate to brief them on the day of the event in an onsite staff briefing. If the event begins early in the morning, there might not be time for an onsite briefing so the staff would attend a pre-event briefing. Or if there are many staff and it would be difficult to take them all aside for an onsite briefing, they would attend a pre-event briefing or be divided across more than one pre-event briefing.

Events with volunteer staff often hold pre-event briefings because there is no cost attached. Also, the nature of an event which utilises volunteers is usually a large event with many volunteers so it is helpful to brief them pre-event.

If The Manager requires paid staff to attend a pre-event briefing, the staff will expect to be paid for their time (and travel) to attend a briefing on a day that is not the event day.

- **Onsite Staff Briefings**

Conducting a briefing to staff onsite on the day of an event is an essential component for customer satisfaction because it is another communication tool for conveying important information to staff such as safety procedures and evacuation routes.

A tour of the venue should be part of the onsite staff briefing for those who are not familiar with the layout – casual staff or agency staff for example. For staff to deliver the best customer service at the event, it is important that they know where the restrooms and the cloakroom are located so they can assist customers quickly and professionally. The worst customer service is for a member of staff to say, "I don't know, I don't usually work here".

Often, onsite staff briefings are considered to be an addition to fit in or a luxury if there is time to do it. But it is important for excellent customer service that the staff are briefed. It should become embedded as a regular and consistent procedure never to be overlooked.

AUTHOR'S VOICE

As part of my onsite staff briefings, I introduce key people – myself as The Manager; my assistant; the head of security in case anybody requires security, and the client so the staff know what the client looks like and they don't refuse to serve them a drink!

I usually brief my staff on key times which customers might ask, such as when the food is being served, when the bar will close, what time the entertainment begins, and what time the event finishes.

I always use the staff briefing to receive questions from the staff. It allows them a voice, and there might be things they want to know which I've overlooked to tell them.

Hotels tend to be complacent with briefings because their duties tend to be repetitive. But it is always good practice to conduct a staff briefing – they do not take long. And if there is not much to say, they take less time! If there is nothing to say, it still goes ahead because that is the embedded procedure – you would not cancel your car service because there is nothing wrong with your car.

Briefings to waiters should happen before every service because staff change, menus change, customers change, and not every service is identical to every other service.

Some hotels forego briefings for repeat events or regular day-to-day events, but again, there is always something to discuss because team members change, and every customer is a different customer.

At events, staff briefings often get 'squeezed' out of the event day because timings do not allow or things fall behind on the schedule. This is an error. A staff briefing only takes between 10 and 20 minutes and must never be omitted from the procedures – even if it means opening the doors late and keeping guests waiting outside.

AUTHOR'S VOICE

At Thorpe Park Resort in Surrey, UK, there was demand from customers for private entertainment such as corporate days out and team-building events utilising the facilities in the park.

But Thorpe Park viewed events as an interruption to the core business of rides, attractions, and entertainment because it was a nuisance when customers wanted to arrive earlier than the public, or stay later, or wanted lunch served in special areas instead of where everybody else would eat lunch.

When I took the role of Head of Events, I implemented communication procedures to enable the work of my events department to be appreciated by the other departments affected by our demanding customers.

I introduced tools of interdepartmental communication such as advance booking notices and event function sheets. I held pre-event operations meetings with other departments for each event so they became involved with planning, safety, finding solutions, and they had engagement and input with how the events would be run.

On the day of an event in the park, I required anybody involved with or affected by the running of an event to attend the onsite briefing so they knew what was happening, where, when, and what it would mean to their day today.

Once the other departments became engaged with events, they understood the revenue being generated and the demands required by the customers we were looking to satisfy, and they became more forgiving and co-operative.

Through these measures of effective interdepartmental communication, I enacted a culture change at Thorpe Park, and with the support of interrelated departments, the events business increased to contribute substantial revenue to the core business.

My objective was to deliver the best customer service our event customers expected, and I needed all the other departments on my side to achieve that goal.

6.4.5 Departmental Communication

Interdepartmental communication is about relations with other departments in a hotel or at an event. Departmental communication is concerned with internal communication within one department.

It is not helpful to have inconsistent procedures across departments because customer service and service efficiency will vary. So, each department should learn the best practices from another. No department should be isolated from another because each department contributes to the goals of the event or hotel: to achieve profit by providing good customer service so that customers have a good experience and will want to return to spend more money which achieves more profit.

It is one thing to have departments communicating with each other, and there are practices which can be introduced to encourage this level of communication, such as staff social events.

But staff within one department should be encouraged to look beyond the boundary of their own department and into the realm of other departments so they can learn what is happening elsewhere and take best practice.

As staff walk through other areas of the event, hotel, or venue, they can be observant. They can be conversant. They can be friendly and ask questions. This will help them import best practice into their home department, and it will develop their own knowledge, skills, and competencies.

Importing best practice to the home department strengthens the team, so The Manager should encourage this to happen. But it must be shared within the department – which is what departmental communication is about.

Teams in a department can often become isolated and will tend to evolve their own traits, practices, and procedures – formally and informally – which introduces gaps between one department's service and another's. The Manager should ensure that their Head of Departments (HODs) are communicating to their respective teams the wider traits, practices, and procedures that are common across the hotel or event to align standards of service and provide a consistent experience for each customer during their journey through the event or hotel.

References

Broom, G.M., and Bey-Ling, S. (2013) *Cutlip and Center's Effective Public Relations*, 11th Ed. Harlow: Pearson Education Ltd.

Shannon, C.E., and Weaver, W. (1963) *The Mathematical Theory of Communication*. Urbana-Champaign: University of Illinois Press.

Chapter 7

Dealing with Complaints

Section 7.1 introduces legislation with complaints under the Trade Descriptions Act which was introduced in 1968.

In Section 7.2, we identify and analyse four types of complainers and suggest how to deal with each type.

Section 7.3 looks at the three states of transactional analysis and its use as a psychological technique to deal with these states of complainers and convert a complainer from one state to another.

Section 7.4 highlights the need to identify whether a complaint is legitimate through the checking procedures and why this is helpful in deciding solutions to resolve any issue. We look at the value of debrief meetings to facilitate ongoing communication in resolving any issues.

In Section 7.5, we present an eight-step guide to complaint handling and then look at the dangers of financial solutions such as discounts and refunds.

Section 7.6 deals with complaints specifically at events to recover service during the point at which it is being consumed by the customer.

DOI: 10.4324/9781003154600-8

Section 7.7 looks at the negotiation and resolution of complaints with a five-point negotiation plan.

In Section 7.8, we show the benefits of recording errors, tracking the outcomes, and which solutions are most effective with the aim to monitor service levels.

Then in Section 7.9, we present two case study examples of actual complaints. The first involves uncooked chicken served at a wedding reception (Section 7.9.1) and the second involves steak preferences at a conference (Section 7.9.2).

7.0 Why Customers Complain

Customers are dissatisfied when their expectations are not met by the event they attend or the hotel they visit.

But when dissatisfaction occurs, it is not a given that customers will always complain.

Some customers are quick to complain. Others may find it embarrassing or are worried about upsetting the staff, so they would rather keep quiet.

Upbringing, culture, personality-type, and history of complaining can each culminate in an overall propensity to complain, hence the phenomena of customers complaining over very trivial errors and others not complaining despite clearly receiving a flawed service.

This presents challenge for The Manager as it can be difficult to gauge how well an event is progressing or how well a hotel is performing because of this variable in terms of propensity to feedback errors.

INDUSTRY VOICE

"I hate Saint Valentine's Night. It's one of those occasions where the expectations are too great and quite a few of your tables are nervous.

I once received a complaint letter after a very successful Valentine's evening where the man had written to say that the food was not to his or his partner's liking to the extent that he decided to not propose to her and 'the ring stayed firmly in my pocket'.

I think that the potential bride was probably relieved".

Andrew Coggings, Managing Director of Hospitality, The Goodwood Estate

The Manager cannot rely solely on freely given customer feedback to make their assessment and should actively encourage all customers to voice their critique.

The reason for this is simple: at the time of the error, it is still possible to make a difference and take steps to mitigate the impacts.

Furthermore, complaints that transpire face-to-face are easier to deal with because of the interpretation of body language, pitch of voice, verbal expression, and visual nuances such as gesticulations and facial expressions.

Handling a complaint online, where the customer might exaggerate and act in a way they never would in person, can be more difficult to handle but will always be too late to recover.

7.1 Legislation of Complaints

Customers for all products and services are protected by the Trade Descriptions Act which was introduced in 1968 and made it an offence for businesses to sell a product or service based on misinformation. The penalties range from fines to imprisonment in severe cases but most often result in compensation being paid to a customer who feels that they have been misled. It was brought into law to prevent businesses from exaggerating the quality of their products with misleading advertisements.

This protection is a difficult area for the event industry as it is more difficult to maintain consistency in terms of the quality of events. Marketeers may advertise an event based on previous years in good faith; yet for a variety of reasons (often out of the control of the business) this time around the quality at the event is reduced. This will cause dissatisfaction and a possible claim under the Trade Descriptions Act if the "disparity is false to a material degree", which has resulted in court cases for some event businesses.

Most customer complaints are dealt with between the customer and the business without ever needing to go to court. Yet, on occasion, it can happen if an agreed compensation cannot be reached. The business must weigh up the time and effort dealing with the case as well as any negative publicity it might generate, before pursuing this path and most likely they will decide to settle. Even a win at court can be a hollow victory after legal expenses are taken into account, hence the need and ability to deal with complaints quickly and efficiently with positive outcomes is an advantage for any event business.

It is much the same for customers – a customer does not want a long and expensive legal battle which they are not even guaranteed to win. All a customer expects is to receive what they were promised. If they did not receive that, they will want redress or compensation but that does not extend to a desire to be in court. Certainly, a customer does not attend an event or stay at a hotel with the aim of ending up in court with The Manager.

Having contracts in place (see Chapter 5, *Contracts*) helps iron out problems before the need to take it to court and used effectively, a contract will deter deviations from agreed services that were put in writing. But even if it does reach court, the contract will assist in the legal process and a judge will look favourably on a contract being in place.

7.2 Types of Complainers

Customers complain for a variety of reasons, from the desire to help a business improve, to looking for compensation. Some complain out of anger or even revenge. It is impossible to know all the motivations behind a complaint.

What is clear is that every customer is different, and multiple customers could have the same experience and some would be disappointed, others might be pleased, some might complain, and others would find it near-impossible to do so.

To assist businesses to deal with a complaint, it is useful to categorise the complainer to help with the approach to take to settle a dispute.

- **Professional Complainer**

  Someone who sees a failure in service as a chance to gain something, either special treatment or compensation. They tend to exaggerate the issue and add other evidence (often trivial) to support their claim and maximise the return. The professional complainer will most likely have experience in complaining and will have received compensation and is now comparing your response with their past conflicts.

  The professional complainer is difficult to deal with as the customer will only be satisfied with compensation and anything less is seen as a failure to resolve. The Manager should remain objective and try to get the customer to at least privately acknowledge that the complaint is exaggerated, but in the end an offer is what will resolve the complaint. The Manager can offer discounts for future service to avoid paying out here and now, or offer something that has value to the customer but costs the business very little, such as a round of drinks, maybe.

- **Prolific Complainer**

  This type of customer has near-zero tolerance for any difference in the quality of what they believe they should have received and what they did actually receive. It can feel as if they are looking for reasons to complain, but they tend to have a strong sense of right or wrong and almost view it as their right and responsibility to highlight an error.

This type of complainer can be easy to deal with as they crave praise and attention. Thanking them for highlighting an issue that can now be fixed to prevent it happening to other customers is a good tactic and will appeal to their sense of doing right. They may settle for less in terms of compensation but only if the complaint is dealt with in a positive way. Rejecting their complaint can result in an extremely negative reaction.

- **Shy Complainer**

This customer struggles with the embarrassment of complaining and is worried about hurting the feelings of staff or causing a fuss. It can be tempting to ignore this type of complainer as they will be exhibiting body language signals that they are not happy, but sometimes never actually complain, and when they do it can be easy to resolve as they will give up quite quickly.

Always try to draw out complaints from the customer rather than let that customer leave, as tempting as it is to let them go. The problem has not gone away, it has most likely gone online instead as a poor review or written complaint. Shy complainers can be much braver behind a keyboard which will then make it much harder to deal with. Yet drawing out the complaint from the customer and dealing with it can create a much more positive outcome.

- **Aggressive Complainers**

This customer exhibits an extreme reaction which does not seem in relation to the actual complaint. Quite often, this is related to something outside the business impacting their experience, such as traffic, or an argument, or even a bad day at work. It can feel like they are taking something out on you rather than focusing on the complaint.

This type of complainer can be emotionally difficult and painful to deal with if taken personally. It can feel very unfair at times and The Manager will need to remember they are representing the business but are not the business itself, so the customer's anger is not directed at them. Finding a way to stay logical and calm and trying not to disagree in any way can calm the customer. Try to get them away from other customers because crowd behaviour can exacerbate a situation, but beware as some customers want to be seen complaining and use it as leverage.

7.3 Transactional Analysis – A Psychological Technique to Deal with Difficult Customers

A well-known and useful technique to deal with angry, upset, or belligerent customers is a psychological process called transactional analysis. It takes advantage of the fact that everything that happens in a person's life has an impact on who they are and how they behave and communicate. Over time, people learn the best way to communicate and will subconsciously adapt to others to be able to do so.

The theory claims that people have the following three states of mind and can change between states at will, depending on circumstances:

- **Parent state**

    This is where people can either be in a caring or judgemental state of mind. It is a common state for complainers as they will be judging the business and exhibiting negative body language and feedback.

- **Child state**

    This is where people are being led by emotions such as playfulness or anger. It can be difficult to deal with someone in this state because they are not thinking in a logical way and so it is imperative to convert them out of this state into another less volatile one.

- **Adult state**

    This is the logical and reasoning state and is the best state to deal with in terms of a complaint. Customers in this state can be reasoned with and placated.

The theory states that people learn over time that the best way to communicate with someone else is to be in the same ego state as the other person. You cannot continue for long in a playful child state if talking to someone in a logical adult state. Yet being in a playful child state with someone who is also being playful, works. Adult state matches with adult, and parent state matches with parent. The exception to this is a parent can converse with a child state, as one defers to the other or cares for the other (Figure 7.1).

This is useful as a technique because if a customer is clearly in either a parent state (being over critical) or a child state (emotional/angry) then remain in your adult state. Stay calm and logical, talk with reason and without emotion, and they will recognise that you are in this state. They then have a subconscious drive

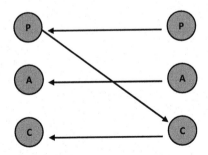

Figure 7.1 Transactional Analysis Matching Series

to also revert to adult as their own personal history tells them that it is the best way to talk to someone in that state. They will move from critical and/or angry to calm and logical.

This may take time to adopt, but it is a highly useful method of calming customers and moving to a state where it is possible to negotiate. Do not allow yourself to become emotional and/or angry as this will mean you are in your child state, and either the angry customer (also in child) or the critical customer (in parent) can both continue in their states.

7.4 Handling Legitimate Complaints

Keep in mind that events and hotels are providing a service which the customer (consumer) is consuming at the point of production, so it is essential to deal with a complaint as it is occurring or before it occurs. If we do not achieve this, our service standards are compromised, the customer receives a lesser experience but most of all it is difficult to recover if that service has already been consumed.

The first step with handling complaints is to identify whether the complaint is legitimate. The best way for The Manager to identify this is by checking. This is why hotel managers walk through the premises speaking to customers and staff to check how their services are performing. It is a social function and demonstrates professional courtesy, but the objective is to understand how customers are receiving the service experience.

It is the same with event managers who have done all the planning before the day of the event, and now, they can check that everything which has been planned is now being performed. During the set-up on the day of an event, The Manager will be checking all areas of the venue such as furniture layout, table set-up, branding, and decoration is in place, the bars are being stocked, the chef is happy in the kitchen, etc. It is all about checking on the day of an event.

Once the set-up is complete but before the doors open for guests, The Manager should tour the venue to perform a final check to ensure that the venue is ready for guests. This check is a safety protocol to ensure that all areas are clean, there is no broken glass or debris, there are no empty boxes or rubbish, emergency escape routes are clear and unobstructed, fire doors are unlocked, there are no trip hazards such as cables or tripod legs.

When the doors are open and the event is happening, The Manager's role is to continue touring the venue to check the performance of the service. This will entail visiting the kitchen to check the foodservice, visiting the bars to check the drinks service, visiting the front door to check the efficiency of guest arrivals and the cloakroom, etc. Then doing it all again.

By constant and consistent checking, The Manager will build a professional assessment of how the service is being performed. This is essential for identifying whether a complaint is legitimate because if a complaint is received, The Manager will already be aware that there was an issue (or not) at that touch point.

If a client has a justified complaint, The Manager should already be aware of the issue through their personal involvement during the event and their checking procedure or by learning about it from other parties during the post-event debriefs. The debriefs eliminate the chance of being surprised by a complaint because other people in the team will inform The Manager if an issue occurred during the event.

Where a customer does raise a complaint, The Manager should be in a position to state that this was already brought to their attention and that they have arranged for the person or supplier who was responsible to learn from it. Thus, a situation can be defended and placated.

AUTHOR'S VOICE

I always conduct client debrief meetings after all the other debriefs (sponsors, venue, suppliers, management team, staff) so that I am fully aware of any issues which might have occurred during the event. This way, I can prepare my defence or think of solutions to propose when I meet the client for their debrief.

If I am aware of an issue and the client raises it at their debrief, I will know that it is a legitimate complaint.

If a client informs me of an issue of which I am unaware because I didn't see it during my checking procedures and none of my debriefs have raised it, I could think it is not a legitimate complaint, and this client is angling for something such as a reduced final bill.

So, knowing the legitimacy of a complaint allows me to think about the solution I offer.

I will still propose a solution for a complaint which may not be legitimate because I want a satisfied client, and it still needs a resolution. Besides, you do have to acknowledge even a made-up complaint and be seen to take it with seriousness. But I am unlikely to offer as much as if it were a legitimate complaint. And, I will possibly choose not to work again with a client who presents a complaint which is not legitimate – but if I do, I will know what to expect next time around.

To be surprised, is a management failure.

Prior knowledge of a complaint allows The Manager to investigate the circumstances and decide what measures to take, such as offering a discount or refund. This is an added value of the debriefing, evaluation, and feedback procedures.

If a customer makes a complaint, The Manager must not avoid any subsequent phone calls or emails. Problems do not go away. Facing the customer to discuss a problem really does work. Where a customer has expressed dissatisfaction, talking to them provides the opportunity for both parties to discuss the situation.

Customers respond well to The Manager who faces the problem, has investigated the situation, and is ready with a proposition.

This is why the scheduling of the client debrief should be arranged before the event happens, to take place after the event (and all debriefs for that matter, because it could be the venue making a complaint or it might be a supplier). Scheduling the debrief meetings ensures that they will go ahead because they are in the diary, and the client is expecting that meeting to happen. Thus, if a complaint does occur, this meeting facilitates the communication process to resolve it. If there are no issues, the debrief simply becomes a catch-up, discussion of how the event went, and is a sales opportunity for future business.

In any case, a debrief extends the client relationship after an event has happened.

INDUSTRY VOICE

"I am amazed how many General Managers delegate complaint letters to their personal assistant, customer services, or anybody who can write an adequate letter and get the General Manager off the hook.

I never let my General Managers do this.

I want complaints to be personally seen by the General Manager and responded to by the General Manager, and if a phone call is required first, then the General Manager must do this.

If a customer has taken the time to put in a written complaint, they deserve a response from the General Manager".

Andrew Coggings, Managing Director of Hospitality, The Goodwood Estate

It is not unknown for customers to invent a complaint to reduce the final bill or receive a refund.

If The Manager has conducted the checking procedures and debriefs, the legitimacy of the complaint will be known.

Even if the complaint is unjustified and The Manager recognises that this is the case, it does not preclude the offer of a compromise or goodwill gesture. It is still good customer service management. But knowing a complaint may not be legitimate allows The Manager to adjust the compromise or goodwill offer to an appropriate level.

If the quality of service has not met with what was advertised or promised, then customers will have a genuine reason for a complaint, depending on the level of disparity.

Some customers are very understanding when this happens, many are not. Some are happy to merely inform the business about the disparity, while others are looking for compensation either in monetary form or additional services.

The method employed to deal with the complaint can significantly impact both what the customer will happily accept as compensation as well as the perception the customer has of the business afterwards.

It is therefore of both monetary and reputational advantage to train and empower staff to deal with complaints (see Chapter 8, *Empowering Staff to Resolve Customer Service*).

7.5 The Eight-Step Method to Dealing with Complaints

1   **Provide the customer with the opportunity to complain in a comfortable way.**

    It can be embarrassing for some customers to have to raise a complaint. Many people struggle with the thought of upsetting staff or making a fuss in front of other customers. Providing a comfortable place to talk is therefore the first stage in the process. It involves the complaint handler taking themselves from the day-to-day business so they can focus on handling the complaint. Making here placating statements such as: "Oh dear, it looks like we have a problem here. Shall we go to the side, I will get you a drink and we can sort this all out, I'm sure" will reassure the customer that their complaint is being taken with the seriousness it merits. It will also warm the relationship with the complimentary drink.

    This also serves to separate the complaining customer away from other customers who might not have been affected by the issue and do not need to be involved. Or, if they experienced the issue as well, it avoids mob-mentality of ganging up. It is better to deal with each complaining customer at a time rather than treat it as a group exercise.

2   Be attentive and give the customer your full attention

Customers will react negatively if they feel their complaint is not being treated with the seriousness it merits. Besides, it is more difficult to handle a complaint if doing so with interruptions. The staff in the vicinity should be informed not to disturb you whilst you are handling the customer.

3   Listen carefully

Try not to jump to assumptions about the complaint. Even when you have knowledge of something which has gone wrong, the customer may have their viewpoint and will still want to get their feelings across to you. In a busy or noisy environment, this can be difficult, but be sure to capture all the details so that the complaint can be handled as well as learn from the error to make sure it does not reoccur.

If it is difficult to deal with the complaint because of a busy or noisy environment, take the customer's contact details and assure them that it will be followed up by you. But if this course is taken, it must be followed through by you and it must be within good time. Otherwise, the complaint will be compounded by your failure to keep that promise.

4   Ask key questions

Bring a pen and notebook to the complaint to record the details. It will help when referring back to the conversation but also it lets the customer know their complaint is being treated with the seriousness it merits.

A tactic is to ask questions whilst the customer gives their version of what happened. This clarifies what happened, but also interrupts the flow of the customer to slow them and calm them. This may seem rude, but short and quick questions are effective in stopping the customer getting carried away and building to a crescendo with their complaint. Some customers will add to the complaint as they go along by finding other minor errors to support their position. A well-timed question can bring them back to the main complaint and stop the customer drifting with their narrative.

5   Agree that a problem exists without accepting liability

This is important to recover the situation but there are complaints from customers that are due to things outside your control (the weather being a common one). You can agree that the "experience you have received isn't what we would have wished", for instance, and does not state that it is the fault of the business.

6   **Apologise for their need to complain**

Until you can establish that the fault is definitely with the business, it is still best to apologise but in a way that satisfies the customer that you are taking the complaint with the seriousness it merits and are sorry they believe they have not received the right experience, without yet admitting to it. A common phrase used is "I am so sorry you aren't satisfied with your experience" or "I'm sorry we haven't met your expectations". Neither admits responsibility.

7   **Investigate and resolve**

This is by far the most difficult step, as you need to decide liability and then choose between several resolution options:

A) Admit the issue is due to a failing of the business and offer compensation to the point that the customer leaves with a positive experience but does not cost the company dearly.

B) Admit the business failed but not to the extent that compensation is required, but a sincere apology and a promise of better service in the future will suffice.

C) Admit the business failed, knowing full well the customer is exaggerating or in error themselves, giving the minimum to the customer to placate them.

D) Dispute the liability and explain to the customer why the difference in service to their expectation is not the fault of the business and risk losing the customer.

Most managers decide options A + B or C and give out large amounts of compensation on a regular basis. The fear of poor reviews and publicity is enough to steer The Manager away from option D. But some stalwarts have been known to stand their ground and argue with the customer (sometimes ending up in the press).

8   **Thank the customer**

It can be difficult for some customers to complain as they tend to feel sorry for the staff member on the end of their complaint. It is important to acknowledge that although unpleasant, feedback is how businesses learn and improve. For this reason, a complaint has been described as a gift to the business. Ensure the customer leaves feeling they have done something positive and contributed to the success of the event or hotel: "Thank you for that feedback, it's good to know when we have missed the mark so we can improve. I really hope to see you next time and we can show you what we can really do".

Giving discounts, refunds, or financial compensation as a resolution is a quick way of keeping the customer quiet but it does not solve anything. First, the customer is already unhappy, and whilst being pacified by receiving a refund, it does not correct the experience they have already received.

Second, refunds, discounts, and financial compensation do not solve the issue that occurred – they only gloss over a problem when it happens.

Remember, discounts, refunds, and compensation affect the profit margin of the event or hotel and go against the purpose of doing business. It is not a solution to continue refunding, discounting, or compensating customers.

It is important to learn from errors so that another customer does not experience the same shortfall in service, and there will be no repeat demands for refunds, discounts, or compensation.

Some managers are too keen to give financial recompense to customers. They may feel that it is an easy way out and then it becomes habitual whenever a customer complains. Discounts and refunds can become the first resort, but it should be the very last resort.

Generously providing refunds, discounts, and compensation creates a reputation spread by word of mouth that this event will refund the ticket price, or this hotel will give money off the bill if the customer complains. It does not take long for one customer to succeed in receiving a discount and tell another customer to do the same.

Instead of giving money out of the business to placate complaining customers, it would be better to offer a discount off their next ticket or bill when the next event happens or the customer returns to the hotel. This provides incentive to the customer and achieves further business even if it is at a discounted rate. It also provides the opportunity for The Manager to demonstrate to the customer that it was a one-off problem and things have now improved.

Of course, it is important to ensure that everything has improved when the customer returns because if they experience a repeat of the issue, it will compound the situation.

Offering complimentary items as a solution is better than offering discounts and refunds. A complimentary drink, coffee, or dessert is a lesser cost to the business. It also allows a little more time to recover the customer by social techniques such as chatting with them or checking up on them that they received their complimentary items and everything is now fine.

Whatever issue caused the complaint, it must be fixed. The customer who complained has raised an awareness of a shortfall in service, so they should be thanked for highlighting the problem for it to be remedied and no other customer will suffer that shortfall, and no other customer will seek financial recompense to the detriment of profits.

INDUSTRY VOICE

"As an operations team we have a system in place whereby all complaints are tracked through our Guest Response procedure.

Each complaint is logged by the member of staff, its outcome and what financial value it has (if any).

These complaints are then categorised on an online log to determine any guest-facing trends.

Each trending complaint then triggers a course of action, i.e. re-training, specification, process.

We review this log in a weekly operations meeting and HODs share the complaints in their team briefings and meetings. The value of the complaint is also logged to determine the financial impact it has.

If our guests have flagged a complaint during their stay, the relevant head of department engages with the guest to ensure their stay was turned around to a positive experience".

Rak Kalidas, Commercial Director, Levy UK

AUTHOR'S VOICE

On the rare occasion I receive a complaint, I challenge myself to make a friend out of the complainer. Sometimes, I think that the more upset a customer is, the better friend they will become!

This is because it takes effort to deal with those who complain, whereas other customers who leave happy don't require that effort. It is a test of personality to win-over customers and it takes powers of experience, social technique, and empathy which I like to practice when a customer complains.

It is very satisfying to win-round a customer who may start from a defensive standpoint but be sociable and friendly once things have been sorted out.

I have customers who were dissatisfied but when I offer them a discount on their next visit, they develop a bond with me. I put it down to the fact that the relationship is already started because they complained. So, when they return, it is an extension of that relationship. I can welcome them back, look after them, make them feel special, give them a complimentary drink, check up on them, and sometimes laugh about what went wrong at their previous visit. It is all about building the customer relationship.

It does mean letting go of proudness, ego, or feelings of superiority. But this is easy because the objective is to have a happy customer, so pride, ego, and superiority aren't things which matter.

7.6 Complaints at Events

Complaints at events are not as easy to resolve as in a hotel. Where a hotel can provide solutions to customers such as inviting them to return for a discounted meal or overnight stay, an event cannot do that because it would already be gone. Events are temporary and the customer is consuming the event at the point of service.

If the event is recurring, such as an annual music festival, it might be possible to provide discounts for the future event or perhaps an associated event if there are other events in The Manager's portfolio. These aside, an issue will require a solution during the event or compensation will need to be provided such as a ticket-price refund, which will impact profits.

The only solution is to not have any complaints! This may sound difficult or impossible, but if The Manager has used the lead-in time for meticulous planning and is conducting checking procedures during the event-build and throughout the event itself, there is no room for error, and every customer will be happy.

Think of it this way: if the stage does not collapse because it was planned and checked, why should customer service fail? It is only that the stage needed to be safe which is why it was planned and checked. If you want customer service to be safe, it needs that level of planning and checking.

Other than not having any complaints, the other solution is to deal with complaints during the event. This requires quick thinking and problem solving.

INDUSTRY VOICE

"When I arrived at Wivenhoe House as the new General Manager, I was made aware of a father of a bride who was disappointed with what he described as the lack of professionalism he had been afforded as they planned his daughter's wedding.

Whilst it is always my first response to support my team, it was clear that my intervention was required to rebuild the relationship, which is exactly what happened.

A meeting was arranged and I was present with my team. At no point did I take over the conversation, but I was able to reassure the Party that their wedding day would have my full attention.

They had a wonderful day and everything went just as planned. That customer and his family have returned on many occasions since".

Oliver Brown, General Manager, Wivenhoe House Hotel

There are direct recovery solutions such as upgrading the customer from a standing ticket to a seated or VIP ticket. Or providing some complimentary products which could be merchandise, drinks, or putting together a goodie-bag for them to take away.

7.7 Negotiating a Resolution

The most difficult part of dealing with a complaint is the negotiation and resolution and it is surprisingly common for staff to skip this part and go straight to compensation. Time must be taken with the complaint to get to the root of the problem as well as understanding the customer and what they want. This will help improve customer service and may mean that the customer is satisfied without receiving anything other than a sincere apology.

The stages of negotiation are:

1 **Preparation**

Join the meeting with the information you need. For example, if staff are trained to always refer a complaint to management, they can take some details first and move the customer to a more private location. Then they can brief The Manager to prepare them for meeting the customer.

It is the difference between being called over to deal with a complaint in a busy lobby, without knowing what the complaint is about or even know the customer's name, or being briefed by a member of staff that Mr Martin is at the bar with a complimentary drink and has a complaint about the way security dealt with him on entry. It allows The Manager to go to security and find out if there was an issue before ever meeting Mr Smith, and then using his name when meeting him.

2   Information

Draw out the complaint in full from the customer using probing questions and compare with the information you have already gathered. Look for common ground (details which agree) and query those which do not. Be attentive and make notes but do not be afraid to challenge. Remember, customers tend to exaggerate to get businesses to take their complaint more seriously.

3   Bargain

Once the facts are agreed, a resolution can be offered depending on company policy and often using discretion and judgement. If the business is at serious fault, then it can be a negotiation about the level of compensation. Whereas if the fault is minor, an apology and a promise to focus on that customer's experience for the rest of their visit are often enough.

Monitor the customer's body language to see how the initial offer is received and use language that allows you to revisit, for example:

It's clear we have failed to deliver our usual level of service. I am so sorry about that and we need to make amends. I was thinking maybe a round of drinks and for me to personally ensure the rest of your visit goes to plan from this point onwards, how does that sound?

This approach allows the customer to respond in a non-confrontational way, for instance: "Well actually this is a special occasion for my family, and it was a bit embarrassing...". This can be added to further the resolution: "Yes of course it is, why don't I see if our chef can make something special for dessert and then we can make a fuss over your family and get this back on track?"

4   Conclude

Summarise at this point so that everyone is clear what has been decided as a resolution and what the business and the customer need to do. This is important as the customer will wish to report back to their friends or family on the outcome and be completely sure that what they tell them is correct.

A thank-you for highlighting the fault is always a good idea, as the customer reporting back that there are no hard feelings and "this was the outcome" is a positive result, compared to them feeling guilty.

5   Execute

Make sure that what was promised is now delivered. If delegating the responsibility to somebody else – complimentary coffees after a meal, for example – The Manager must check to ensure that this has been handled and it gives the chance to check on the customer which they will further appreciate.

The most difficult complaint to deal with is where the original complaint has been mishandled. Trust is lost, and the outcome will likely be expensive.

7.8 Possible Complaint Outcomes

After a complaint has been resolved, it is useful to record the error and the outcome to identify frequent or recurring mistakes and the level of complaints as well as levels of compensation and which solutions are most effective.

It can be useful to categorise these complaints and track the outcomes using a sliding scale measure to help monitor quality (Table 7.1).

The importance here is that a skilled customer service agent can often resolve more serious complaints with lower outcomes. Whereas dealing with a complaint badly can have the reverse effect.

The example below highlights a critical complaint outcome which must have come from a major or even a medium complaint which would need investigating. Depending on the size of the business, the tracking process can be much more complicated or just a tally system. But most businesses have some way of monitoring errors, as unpleasant as the process can seem.

7.9 Case Study Examples of Actual Complaints from the Event Industry

The two case studies below are examples of how a skilled member of staff can deal with a serious complaint which was the fault of the business but had a positive outcome and how an inexperienced staff member can do the reverse:

7.9.1 Case Study 1 – Uncooked Chicken Served at a Wedding

Background – The event is a wedding taking place in a hotel with 100 guests and a reasonably complex menu and service style. The bride arrives earlier than expected but the service staff cope well, and the welcome drinks are ready, as are the starters, table wine, etc. Unfortunately, the main course with breast of chicken that had been only sealed (slightly cooked on the outside to hold in the flavour, to be finished off before service) is sent out raw in the middle. The bride's father on the top table (always served first) is the first to notice and speaks to the waiter who then tells The Manager at haste.

Table 7.1 Categorisation and Tracking of Complaint Outcomes

Complaint Severity	Mild	Medium	Major	Critical
Definition	An error which had minimum impact, for example, long queue to enter the venue.	An error which had an impact on the overall quality of the event, for example, sound system error during the event.	An error which had a significant impact on quality and will likely lead to the customer never returning, for example, room overheated to a distressing level.	A significant error which impacted multiple customers and caused multiple complaints, for example, food poisoning.
January	15	4	1	0
%	75	20	5	0
Complaint Outcomes	Mild	Medium	Major	Critical
Definition	Apology acceptance and promise of future service	Apology acceptance and compensation below £50	Apology acceptance and compensation above £50 with possible negative PR	Apology non-acceptance, not resolved with possible written complaint, bad PR and legal action
January	17	2	0	1
%	85	10	0	5

At the Table:

BRIDE'S FATHER TO WAITER – "What the hell are you playing at, this chicken is raw!" pointing at the freshly cut chicken, clearly uncooked.

WAITER – "Oh my goodness, I am so sorry, let me take that back. I will get the Manager as this is very serious, thank you so much for spotting it".

Waiter rushes to The Manager in the kitchen.

WAITER – "The bride's father says his chicken is raw and it definitely is, I can see the blood".

THE MANAGER – "Take all the plates off the table and ask if any guests have eaten any of the chicken".

WAITER – "There's no way, you can see the blood".

THE MANAGER – "Ask anyway just to be sure, and it might help us deal with this later to be able to say we know nobody has eaten any. Is it Mr Jones, sitting to the right of the bride?"

WAITER – "Yes".

THE MANAGER – "Okay. Halt the kitchen, and get those plates back, leave the rest to me. If any customer asks about it, admit there is a problem, and Mr Jones is dealing with it with the Manager. Otherwise, others will join in complaining".

WAITER – "Okay, no problem".

(The Manager now has the name of the guest, the issue, and in this case, the certainty that it is the business at fault. They also know that the issue has been stopped from spreading and nobody is in danger.)

The Manager to Mr Jones (plates are being removed)

THE MANAGER (REMAINING CALM IN ADULT STATE) – "Good afternoon Mr Jones, would it be possible to talk at the bar, we clearly have a problem and I would like to resolve it and make amends as soon as possible so that it doesn't disrupt the day".

MR JONES – "I should bloody think so!" *Moves to the bar.*

(The Manager needs to get Mr Jones away from the bridal party or they would join their voices to the dispute and make it much harder to resolve. Mr Jones moves because he wants to deal with this away from the bride.)

The Manager to Mr Jones

THE MANAGER – "Let me get you a drink, Mr Jones. That must have been quite a shock. Jerry can you get Mr Jones a...".

MR JONES – "Scotch, please".

THE MANAGER – "Let me begin by saying how sorry I am this happened, it's really unforgiveable and actually dangerous as well".

(It is pointless to try to argue the error, so it is better to admit the failing and the repercussions rather than allow Mr Jones to do the same in an exaggerated way.)

MR JONES – "You could have killed someone!"

THE MANAGER – "Exactly sir, and we by law need to report this occurrence and will do so by the end of the day. I will deal with that. But it's more important to me right now that I recover this event for your daughter so it doesn't spoil her day".

MR JONES (finding it difficult to remain angry with The Manager in adult calm state) – "Okay, but I think this is outrageous!"

THE MANAGER – "Yes, it is, it's the only time in my 10 years at the hotel that anything like this has ever happened".

(It is always useful to get this statement out as it reassures the customer that this is an unusual error and they have been very unlucky.)

THE MANAGER – "I am therefore authorised to do anything in my power to make this up to you, so what I have done is call up the chefs from our restaurant to help redo every dish, which I will check personally, and the chef who sent out the food will face a disciplinary and has been sent home. They are also adding some extras from the main restaurant menu. To prevent your guests having to wait we have added an extra course which you can see going to tables right now".

(As luck would have it, there is soup from the restaurant ready, and to fill the time gap, the chef agrees to send this out immediately.)

THE MANAGER – "I would also like to invite the whole top table back for a complimentary meal in our restaurant so that we can show you what we can do on a great day, perhaps a birthday?"

MR JONES – "Okay..."

(Inviting guests to return is always a good tactic as it costs less than compensation and gives the chance to recover your reputation.)

THE MANAGER – "Oh, and please don't concern yourself with the top table's bar bill, I have zeroed the drinks and will personally make sure you don't buy a drink all night as a thank you for spotting the issue and stopping what could have been a catastrophic error on our part".

(The language here suggests there is no harm done and it has been resolved, while rewarding Mr Jones for being the one who spotted the error.)

Mr Jones returns to the top table and boasts to the bride and groom that he has sorted it all out, the extra course was down to him, and food was coming from the "fancy restaurant" now and the chef who sent the food was sacked (not true). He says the drinks were all free now too and that the "boss man" is checking every dish before it goes out (he never mentions his own free drinks and gets rather drunk this night) and that they could all come back for free on his birthday.

The incident is resolved and when it is reported to Environmental Health, Mr Jones assists the hotel by confirming that nothing was eaten, and it was dealt with well. There is no negative PR (possibly because Mr Jones has minimal memory of it the next day) and the cost to the business is around £250. The alternative would be a possible full refund for a wedding of £10,000 if it had gone to Trading Standards, plus significant damage to reputation.

7.9.2 Case Study 2 – Steak Preferences at a Conference

Background – at a conference dinner for 200 delegates, through poor menu design, an event allows customers to choose how they would like their steaks cooked. This overwhelms and confuses the staff and some steaks are sent out to the wrong people either overcooked or undercooked.

At the Table:

DELEGATE TO WAITER – "Excuse me, I asked for rare and this looks well-done to me".
WAITER – "Oh okay, I think a few people have complained about this as well, I will get someone when I get a chance".

(Best not to volunteer that others are complaining and the "when I get the chance" escalates the complaint.)

Waiter to The Manager in the kitchen

WAITER – "There's another guy who says his steak is overcooked".
THE MANAGER (AGITATED ALREADY) – "For goodness' sake, did you get the plate back?"
WAITER – "Haven't had time, no".
THE MANAGER – "Great thanks.... What's his name, and what table is he on?"
WAITER – "Table 3, I think. Didn't catch his name, he is a big guy in a blue suit".

(The Manager approaches the wrong person who also then wants his steak changed, he eventually got the waiter to point out the original complainer.)

THE MANAGER *(AGITATED IN CHILD STATE)* – "Sorry sir, it has been really busy today, can I help you, James said there was a problem?"

DELEGATE – "There was yes ... but I got someone else to swap my steak now".

THE MANAGER – "Oh okay, that's good then". *Turns to leave.*

(Never assume the complaint is over, read the body language and get the details.)

DELEGATE *(STARTED IN ADULT, HAS NOW FLIPPED TO CHILD AND IS ANGRY)* – "Hang on a minute! I shouldn't have to fix this myself, you were supposed to, the least you could do is say sorry".

THE MANAGER *(CLEARLY ANNOYED)* – "Fine ... sorry, happy now?"

The delegate does not verbally complain anymore but describes this occurrence to not just his table because he is also the conference organiser. He also posts it on his social media and Trip-Advisor under "rude, incompetent staff" which drops the average for the conference venue. The conference books elsewhere the year after. The cost to the business is a lost booking worth over £12,000.

Chapter **8**

Empowering Staff to Resolve Customer Service Issues

In this chapter, we look at why it is beneficial for staff to be empowered to recover customer service when issues arise. The chapter sets out with explaining a system of limits to control the level of staff empowerment when dealing with complaints so they can do so within comfortable parameters. We then look in turn at the benefits of staff empowerment from the perspectives of staff (Section 8.1), managers (Section 8.2), customers (Section 8.3), and the business (Section 8.4).

The aim for any issue that arises is to provide a swift and acceptable solution.

8.0 The Benefits

Staff are frontline receivers of complaints or incidents as they occur, so it makes sense for them to be empowered to handle these incidents. They are in the best and ideal position to deal with the situation calmly and quickly before it becomes an enlarged problem by delay, frustration, or bringing more people into the situation.

It is often the case that staff will already have some level of rapport with the customer, or they know the background to the situation and are fully capable

DOI: 10.4324/9781003154600-9

and prepared to deal with the situation, or they have encountered this situation previously and have experience in how to approach the solution. A manager or supervisor, however, is typically one step removed which does not make them the best person to deal with a situation.

In any case, if the customer and staff are already in conversation about an issue, it is already in progress and should move along to conclusion. It does not help to bring in another party such as a supervisor or manager to return to the beginning by having to explain everything again. This will only delay the solution, frustrate the customer, and undermine the staff.

There is no reason for staff not being empowered to deal with a situation if limits or levels of empowerment have been set for staff to know how far they can go in resolving the issue or what they can offer the customer. Thus, there is no risk.

For staff empowerment to happen effectively, there needs to be a determined range of parameters which allow for a member of staff to comfortably deal with situations. Here is an example:

Example:

In a restaurant situation where a customer complains that the food service is too slow, the service staff could be given the following empowerment limits:

Level of Complaint

Level 1 Mild complaint: Apologise

Level 2 Strong complaint: Apologise, offer complimentary coffee

Level 3 Very strong complaint: Apologise, offer complimentary bottle of house wine

Level 4 Exceptional complaint: Apologise, offer 15% discount voucher for next meal

If the customer is unhappy with what you offer within your limits of empowerment, or requests further recompense, call the head of department or duty manager.

In the above example, staff are aware of what they are permitted to offer in four levels of complaint.

First, staff should be trained to identify whether the complaint is justified. This is usually easy to determine because staff are the people who know if things are running well or not. If there is indeed a problem during the service period, staff will be aware the foodservice is slow, say, and therefore a complaint received from a customer would be deemed justified. Here, they could offer Level 3 or 4 as a solution because they know there was a service failure. A manager who is one-step removed would have to first identify whether the complaint is justified which would take the issue back to the beginning by conducting an exploratory investigation with the staff.

If staff feel it is not a justified complaint – probably because they did not identify any failures during service – they would offer the Level 1 or Level 2 solution to keep the customer content and show they are doing something to rectify the customer's dissatisfaction. This is a solution to satisfy the customer. It is not to tell them their complaint is not justified or arguing with them about whether it is justified or not.

Remember, the objective of good customer service is to keep the customer happy. It is not a solution to determine whether their complaint is justified.

The purpose of determining whether a complaint is justified is to understand which solution to provide. It is not to argue with the customer to prove or disprove their complaint (see Chapter 7, *Dealing with Complaints*).

If a situation has previously occurred to cause customer dissatisfaction and is likely to do so again – a repetitive situation – it is easier to set the levels of staff

---

INDUSTRY VOICE

"All team members should be empowered to ensure customers have a positive experience and that any issues are resolved effectively.

In many organisations, management teams display a lack of trust with their teams. This can sometimes be because they haven't recruited and developed their teams effectively and therefore know they are not in a strong position to best understand and resolve situations. Customers don't want to have to wait for a manager, they want their problems to be fixed. By giving all team members the ability and empowering them to do this, not only is it better for the customer but also helps to build trust in your team and improve the employee experience".

Adam Rowledge, Managing Director, Rowledge Associates

empowerment from previous experience and knowledge of the situation. Here, staff are helpful with identifying repeat complaints they receive and offering their ideas for solutions which they feel would satisfy customers. The range of levels of empowerment to deal with customer dissatisfaction or complaints and proportionate solutions can be decided this way.

Of course, the objective of good customer service is for complaints not to happen at all. If a situation is repetitive, it must be understood why it is rehappening, and steps must be introduced to prevent it from recurring.

Finding solutions for complaints and setting levels of empowerment are not substitutes for providing poor customer service. They are tools to enact if a complaint does occur so that staff can deal with the situation in a confident, professional, and immediate way.

It is difficult to understand why staff would not be empowered within acceptable limits or levels. But it is a common problem at events and in hotels for staff not to be empowered.

Without empowerment, staff are being forced to stand in front of a customer and receive a complaint – most often, it is a repetitive complaint which they could easily handle – but are not permitted to resolve the issue and must instead 'call a manager'.

Finding a supervisor, head of department, or duty manager delays the solution, takes time and productivity from staff to find a manager and communicate the issue, and takes time and productivity from the supervisor or manager in having to deal with the issue, which the staff member could have handled in the first instance.

INDUSTRY VOICE

"Motivating staff to be customer focused has to be cultural in the first place. Employ people who genuinely care about the customer experience. Make sure the customer experience successes are shared within the organisation and celebrated widely.

Reward people for doing it right – from a thank-you to mini-incentives, through to major incentives.

Study the customer journey. How organisationally can you enhance it? Involve the teams in this. Basically, live and breathe the customer experience and everything will follow".

Danny Pecorelli, Managing Director, Exclusive Collection

8.1 The Benefits for Staff

Empowerment allows staff to gain experience and development in the job they are doing and the career they are forging. It provides them with confidence in handling customers and situations, and it helps develop soft skills (social skills) such as communication, customer service, complaint handling, and problem solving. Staff want to develop in their role and they like to feel they are doing a good job by delivering the best customer service and receiving praise from their superiors for doing so. Empowering staff to make limited decisions in their job role fulfils their needs.

Staff also want satisfaction from resolving issues. This is recognition of their efforts in doing a good job. This requires reflection from customers, other staff, and their manager in the form of praise, reward, and motivation. Taking these opportunities away because staff have been instructed to call a manager to deal with problems goes against good practice. It also insinuates mistrust and that they are not capable of dealing with customers and resolving issues.

INDUSTRY VOICE

"Whilst there must be parameters set around what allowances can be made, all members of the team must be given the authority to deal with a complaint through immediate action to resolve the issue either through replacement or refund.

Staff must be trusted and empowered to take the appropriate action to resolve an issue as swiftly and as professionally as possible".

Andrew Coggings, Managing Director of Hospitality, The Goodwood Estate

---

8.2 The Benefits for Management

If staff are empowered to deal with customer situations and complaints, managers do not get tied up with operational issues which a capable member of staff could remedy.

It is often seen as a manager's responsibility to deal with complaints but if staff are able to do so, why should a higher-paid member of the team be tied up with these solvable situations – especially so, if the complaint is repetitive.

Deflecting issues to managers does not resolve the problem, it only shifts it up the organisational structure. The real issue for managers is why problems are

> ### INDUSTRY VOICE
>
> "We are a people industry. We cannot do everything ourselves, so we have to ensure that immaculate service is given by everybody who has an interaction with a guest and to do this is far more difficult than people think.
>
> The secret therefore is recruiting and then retaining great staff and constantly developing them and gradually empowering them so that they take ownership of their roles to a greater extent as they grow and accept more responsibility".
>
> *Andrew Coggings, Managing Director of Hospitality, The Goodwood Estate*

occurring – what went wrong and how can it be fixed not to happen again. This is what managers should be focusing on more than the immediate resolution of an isolated incident. It is not a manager's job to jump in every time there is an issue, but it is a failure of management not to fix the problem.

Managers should be in a position of leadership where they develop and motivate their staff to do the best job in the most productive way. Taking empowerment away from staff will stifle their development, motivation, and skills which in turn reduces productivity and good levels of customer service. This will generate complaints and the cycle continues.

Managers should not need or want to intervene with every complaint that interrupts their other management responsibilities of higher priority.

It is not a priority for managers to sort out problems, it is their priority to prevent problems from happening in the first place – that is the job of management.

8.3 The Benefits for Customers

Customers do not want to complain. They only want the experience for what they are paying and for their expectations to be met.

If somehow the customer experience is misaligned with their perceptions such as value for money or their expectations of service, quality or facilities, they might (and should) complain.

INDUSTRY VOICE

"Our operations team are empowered as part of the Guest Response model to deal with complaints at point of contact.

A service recovery model is in place whereby the associate is able to make key decisions on ensuring guest satisfaction is achieved (escalated, dependent on the recovery model).

As part of the escalation procedure there is follow-up from the supervisory and management team. All post-stay complaints are handled by the Guest Relations team who liaise with the relevant head of department to respond, too.

All complaints are logged under the guest profile to ensure the guest is highlighted on future visits".

Rak Kalidas, Commercial Director, Levy UK

When a customer does complain, they want it resolved quickly and easily with the minimum of fuss. Fuss and delay increase frustration and add fuel to the initial complaint.

The last thing a customer wants when they already feel wronged is for a staff member to ask them to wait for a manager. It demonstrates everything we are trying to avoid: poor leadership of staff, lack of professionalism, delay, and fuss.

The quickest, easiest way to deal with a complaint – and to minimise fuss and frustration – is to have the issue dealt with at the point of complaint. The staff are at the point of complaint. They are in the best position to meet all the objectives of dealing with customers: quickly, quietly.

Customers will often understand that a problem is not the fault of the person who is serving them, whether it is a receptionist, waiter, or room attendant. Customers are prone to show empathy with the 'worker' who is only trying to do their job. They'll say, "I know it is not your fault, but…" or "I'm not having a go at you, but…". This stance is helpful when sorting out problems because if the staff are empowered, the customer will feel even better towards that staff member if he or she is able to resolve the issue.

The goodwill and empathy a customer might feel towards staff is not always transferred to a manager when the manager is called upon to step in. Often, the manager will find it more difficult to deal with the situation because the issue has already escalated only by the fact that they have been called to deal with it.

8.4 The Benefits for the Business

Businesses want to run smoothly. They need to be productive and efficient. The objectives of any business are to gain customers, retain them for repeat business, and achieve profit. This can only be achieved by keeping customers happy during their experience of their visit to the hotel or event.

Empowering staff to make decisions within limited parameters meets all the objectives a business sets out to achieve:

(smooth running + productivity and efficiency + great customer service = happy customers) = profit

Take staff empowerment out of the equation of running the business, and the business falters.

Staff feel mistrusted or frustrated at not being allowed to resolve situations they know they could solve. They are prevented from the rewards and motivation of doing their job to the best of their ability. They become dissatisfied and unhappy.

'Suddenly' the business is not achieving the objectives it set out to achieve. The term 'suddenly' is used here not because it happens quickly. It happens over time. But the realisation that the business is faltering is sudden only when it has become obvious. By which time, it is already too late because the problems are already embedded in the practices of the business.

It is extremely difficult to change procedures, retrain staff, re-motivate staff, recover a tarnished reputation of staff and customers, and rebuild clientele.

If staff are unhappy, they will leave which increases staff turnover. Recruiting for replacement staff costs money to advertise, interview, and train which impacts negatively on profit, productivity, and efficiency.

Staff turnover also impacts negatively on service standards because when the business is understaffed, it cannot deliver what has been promised to the customer.

Whilst new staff are learning the job and are under training and settling in, service and quality are below where they should be.

Being understaffed and having demotivated staff equals compromised levels of efficiency, productivity, and service. Customers will not be happy about this.

> ## INDUSTRY VOICE
>
> "Healthy relationships are based on trust and engender an empowered and engaged team.
>
> Team-members should be trusted to handle complaints and to seek help from management to help them solve it if needed.
>
> This style of inverted hierarchy gives confidence to the team-member rather than disempowering them and breeds more engagement to build a happy team all wanting to make a difference to the customer.
>
> A happy team makes happy customers therefore always, where possible, empower your staff to solve issues by themselves".
>
> *Sally Beck, General Manager, Royal Lancaster Hotel, London*

They will complain. Refunds are made which further impacts profit. Reputation will suffer ... All this because The Manager was frightened to empower staff – even with levels of limitation in place.

Businesses benefit from staff who are empowered to make decisions. Providing limits for the decisions staff can make is acceptable because control needs to be maintained by management. Staff do not want responsibility to make big decisions – that is not what they are being paid to do, and they do not want to be responsible for making wrong decisions that cost the business. This is where empowerment limits work because they provide flexibility and balance whilst maintaining control of running the business.

Managers and staff are a team and should work together towards the goals of the business. There is no risk in providing staff with levels of empowerment – it is fully controllable. As long as the staff are aware they can at any time refer to a manager if they are unhappy to deal with a situation, or if they are unsure, or if the customer requires a resolution above the level of staff empowerment.

It is important for staff to record complaints received and the solutions provided so that The Manager can see what problems are occurring, how frequently they are occurring and which solutions are being provided. If staff are being empowered to make decisions with limits, it cannot be handed over without monitoring – if three bottles of wine are being given out each day to compensate customers, it would be a problem.

INDUSTRY VOICE

"I find that allowing all staff to deal with complaints is most effective within our business. We are a small team and often there isn't a manager present.

For this to work we have set boundaries around the level of compensation a team member is able to give in any situation. This has instilled a level of confidence in my team to handle things without my involvement".

Dan Gatehouse, General Manager, Victorian House Hotel, Grasmere

---

Empowerment is not about complacency, passing the buck, or managers feeling they are too busy to deal with day-to-day problems. It is a management strategy to meet the objective of recovering excellent customer service in situations where it falls short.

8.5 Servant Leadership to Increase Employee and Customer Satisfaction

This section is contributed by Maroun E. Aouad and provides an overview of the main concepts of servant leadership, employee satisfaction, and customer satisfaction. The relationships among these pertinent concepts are also developed based on the existing academic literature and industry news and practices.

It is important to understand how customer satisfaction is impacted by the style of leadership and the competency of the leader.

It is all very well to empower employees but this will only happen with some leaders, depending on their style of leadership and the competency of the leader.

Leadership is the ability to mobilise and influence others to do something, and therefore, it greatly affects the performance of a group and has a vital role in organisations and their operations. A simple yet specific definition of leadership can be a process whereby a group of individuals is influenced by the leader to work to attain a mutual goal.

Today's employees are at the cliff face of a new work environment. Employees will not just follow blindly, obey orders, and operate with absolute loyalty. Nowadays employees search meaningfulness in their jobs as well as many other aspects of their life. The events, hotel, and hospitality industries are moving from the conventional autocratic leadership model to a more participatory style in which decision-making is shared. Continuing to move from traditional hierarchical models of leadership, a more caring, ethical, and participatory method of leadership emerges. Whilst not a new leadership theory, *Servant Leadership* may be a theory of this present time and specifically in the service industries.

Greenleaf (1970) coined the term 'servant leadership' in his essay titled, *The Servant as Leader*:

The servant-leader is servant first ... It begins with the natural feeling that one wants to serve, to serve first. Then conscious choice brings one to aspire to lead ... The difference manifests itself in the care taken by the servant-first to make sure that other people's highest priority needs are being served. The best test, and difficult to administer, is this: Do those served grow as persons? Do they, while being served, become healthier, wiser, freer, more autonomous, more likely themselves to become servants? And what is the effect on the least privileged in society? Will they benefit or at least not be further deprived?

Servant leadership was initiated by Greenleaf who believed that the roles of servant and leader, although a paradoxical concept, could occur within one person. According to Greenleaf, a leader's greatness comes from being a servant to others, altruistically, that having empathy and full acceptance of others are what form great leadership. Moving from self-orientation, being an altruist and moral person fits a servant leader and requires a strong character, self, emotional, and psychological maturity. The servant leader recognises and prioritises the needs of others, their interests, goals, individually, and above those of their own. In return, the followers trust the servant leader.

The concept of servant leadership is distinct from any other leadership type as it emphasises the interests of others inside and outside the organisation. The leader's duty is to assume moral responsibility for their subordinates, customers, and stakeholders. In other words, servant leaders take care of their entrusted followers, empower them, and commit to their well-being development whilst ensuring the concern towards others within the organisation, the customers, and the larger community.

Characteristics: listening, empathy, healing, awareness, persuasion, conceptualisation, foresight, stewardship, commitment to the growth of people, and building community.

In practice, the servant-first leader is an extremely different type of the leader-first. The latter is a power-led leader who follows the traditional hierarchical leadership as shown in Figure 8.1 below. Under this type of leadership, the leader acts from a position power drive and obtains material possessions to command

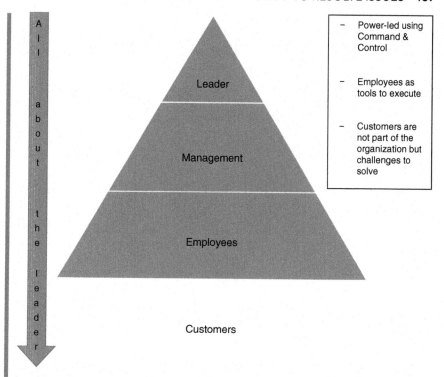

Figure 8.1 Traditional Leadership Hierarchy Challenges

and control the entire operation through using employees as tools to execute and follow orders and respond to customers' challenges.

However, the behaviours and practices of the servant leader flip the hierarchy chart upside down (see Figure 8.2). Instead of being all about the leader, it is all about the people. In other words, the servant leaders as a hotel general manager put themselves in service of the people to inspire and support them to emphasise collaboration and develop trust, empathy, and the ethical use of power. This practice is focused on a desire to serve others and enhance employees' growth, teamwork, and overall employee and customer satisfaction.

Practitioners have been attempting to discover the most effective leadership style not only to meet the organisational service goals efficiently and effectively but also to keep the followers motivated, satisfied, and to serve their needs, and all other stakeholders (i.e., employees, customers, and communities).

Among many leadership styles, specifically for the hospitality industry, servant leadership is regarded as an effective leadership style. Servant leadership is

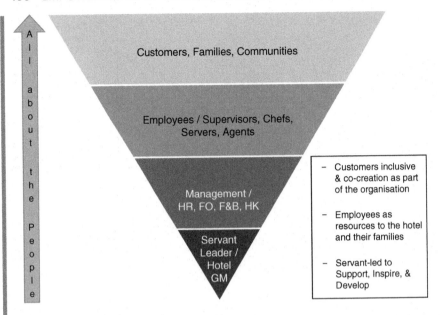

Figure 8.2 Servant Leadership Hierarchy

believed to improve collaboration and encourages employees to achieve service excellence and supports more morality-centred and inspirational self-reflection by leaders than other leadership styles.

In the practical world, adding to the proposition that 'Servant leaders practice leadership as hospitality', the list of companies within the *100 Best Companies to Work For* that are practicing servant leadership and have it within their core

---

INDUSTRY VOICE

"When you join the Royal Lancaster London, you have joined a hotel that cares about your career progression, you have not just taken a job. We pride ourselves in helping our team members and colleagues become the very best that they can be.

We have one of the best apprenticeship records in London and have been voted in The Times Top 100 Best Companies to Work For, by our employees for 4 years running & Best Employer by Springboard in 2018".

Sally Beck, General Manager, Royal Lancaster Hotel, London

business philosophy is increasing, for example: Starbucks, Darden Restaurants, Chick-fil-A, Marriott International, Ritz Carlton, Kimpton Hotels & Restaurants, and Royal Lancaster London Hotel.

8.5.1 Servant Leadership – Employee Satisfaction

One of the main challenges facing hospitality organisations has always been and still is to retain employees. Finding qualified employees and keeping them is an existing problem in the hotel and event industries. Ensuring that staff are satisfied with their job is becoming important to retain them and make them more committed and engaged. Job satisfaction is the degree to which employees like and are satisfied in their jobs. As an attitudinal variable, employee satisfaction captures the global feeling of employees liking or disliking their jobs.

In general, when hotels or events employees assess their satisfaction at work, they evaluate if they are happy with the work they do and if they are frequently thinking to quit or not. Having said that, a happy employee will not think to quit the workplace. Such an employee enjoys coming to work every day to deliver a high-quality service to their customers. Satisfied employees can be more committed and related to the organisation and maintain high service quality and increase customer loyalty.

Leadership has been identified as a major element in the managerial role of managers. New leadership behaviours are currently in high demand for more people-centred (employee, customer) and ethical management practices to motivate the 21st-century workforce specifically in hospitality firms seeking to distinguish themselves. As a result, organisations are struggling to stay competitive due to many challenges.

Mainly, employees are losing trust in their leaders and have no appetite for ego-centric, self-centred leaders (refer to Figure 8.1). Additionally, the centred management style is an important source of frontline employees' dissatisfaction. At the same time, the ethical leader pool is shrinking, and many employees have little to no commitment to organisations. All this leads to dissatisfied and disengaged employees therefore to high employee turnover which is still the most common problem the hospitality industry is suffering. Moreover, attracting, maintaining, and motivating frontline hospitality staff is a key role of successful operations but remains a big issue for hospitality organisations.

That is, a core characteristic of servant leadership, selflessness, or looking beyond the interest of oneself, as explained earlier, could be the answer to employees when they are concerned about how their managers treat them showing non-abusive supervisory behaviours which make them respected followers and more committed to the organisation.

Not surprisingly, employees who recognise that their leaders show servant leadership behaviours such as forming long-term relationships with them, understand, empathise, and putting their interests first, work with them to grow and develop, empower them, and display ethical behaviours feel more satisfied in their job.

INDUSTRY VOICE

"Implementing servant leadership in the philosophy and core values of the hotel management is what differentiates our hotel working environment.

We care about all employees and make sure that everyone is included in the meetings to be heard, and listen to everyone's idea. We put their needs first and support them to develop.

Therefore, all our employees are happier and prouder to work in the Royal Lancaster Hotel. I can say that the employee turnover rate is decreasing and we are able to retain our people".

Sally Beck, General Manager, Royal Lancaster Hotel, London

8.5.2 Servant Leadership – Customer Satisfaction

For better results, hotel leaders must understand how their leadership would affect not only the attitudes of their employees but the outcomes on their customers in the workplace, too.

At customer level, satisfaction is considered one of the most critical factors influencing customers' future behaviour and has always been an organisational goal, especially in the highly competitive hotel industry.

Oliver (1980) explained the expectation/disconfirmation paradigm and clarified that consumers grow their expectations about a product or service before purchase and then they compare actual performance to those expectations after purchase to define their satisfaction (or dissatisfaction) with the purchase. Later, he explored the equity model. The model elucidated that when consumers receive more value in terms of price, time, and effort that they actually spent, satisfaction would exist.

In his book, customer satisfaction (CS) is defined as follows:

Satisfaction is the consumer's fulfilment response. It is a judgment that a product/service feature, or the product or service itself, provided (or is providing) a pleasurable level of consumption-related fulfilment, including levels of under- or over- fulfilment.

In the restaurant industry, customers are more satisfied when perceived high quality and value in terms of service, food, and price, in addition to the overall experience that would likely affect their intention to come back or recommend the place to others.

As customers have more information about a hotel rating and type, their expectations of their stay will build accordingly, and they compare it to their actual stay experience afterwards.

Although the different types of hotel businesses and the wide diversity of customer profiles make it challenging to satisfy, leaders and their employees must work to meet their needs and to exceed their expectations.

In practice, taking the restaurant business as an example, both the followers (employees) and other resources within the organisation such as the customers of the restaurant will cultivate the behaviours of the servant-led leader (manager/supervisor).

A servant leader, the restaurant manager in this case, will be listening attentively as an important part of the verbal and non-verbal communication. When the manager or supervisor in the restaurant listens with empathy to every request or complaint by any customer as well as practicing the same skills with their team members, they are more likely to be trusted. Customers will feel more comfortable in such surroundings where they can ask for any dining service knowing that they will be delivered to their needs and expectations.

At the same time, the servant leader, the supervisor in this case, is the one who is taking care of the day-to-day operations whilst keeping balance in thinking about the long-term effect and objectives of the restaurant reflecting the conceptualising characteristic of a servant leadership mentioned earlier.

The supervisor makes sure that all the needs of the customers will be met, and that they are satisfied with the food, the service, and having an enjoyable experience by always being around and directly in contact with them.

This leader knows very well that this kind of care and behaviour will lead to increased guest satisfaction, and these guests will come back and tell other people about their good experience. Keeping this in mind, by practicing stewardship, a characteristic of servant leadership, the supervisor in this restaurant will be committed to serve the needs of others including the employees and the customers and will be holding the trust for their and the community's best experience.

Those happy customers will always feel this trust and belonging to the community, and they will be willing to share their suggestions for improvement with the staff and the leader. Moreover, they will reflect positive words and stories about their experience to relatives, friends, and other customers.

Those happy employees will feel this care and stewardship which creates a good relationship with their supervisors to cater to their needs and makes them happier and ready to share their satisfaction while providing a better service quality. Therefore, increasing the satisfaction level of the employees will lead to more satisfied customers under the management of a servant-led leader.

8.5.3 The Service-Profit Chain

Service organisations' management centre of concern has been the value creation from both employees and customers to increase profitability resulting from the right operating strategy and resources investment at management level.

In the early 1990s, a team of researchers from Harvard Business School proposed a model for the first time linking the management resources and practices, employees, quality of service, customers, and organisational performance. Heskett et al. (1994) presented and put into work the Service-Profit Chain (SPC) model framework (Figure 8.3).

The organisational strategy of the model, as they defined it, moves backwards starting from the end of the SPC towards its beginning:

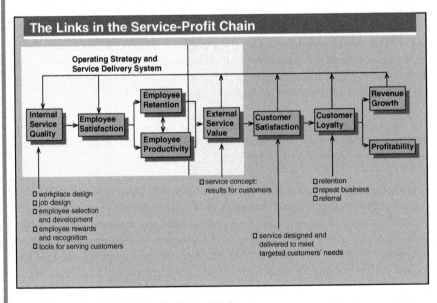

Figure 8.3 The Service-Profit Chain (SPC)

Profit and growth are stimulated primarily by customer loyalty. Loyalty is a direct result of customer satisfaction. Satisfaction is largely influenced by the value of services provided to customers. Value is created by satisfied, loyal, and productive employees. Employees' satisfaction, in turn, results primarily from high-quality leadership support services and policies that enable employees to deliver results to customers.

The SPC allows managers to look at the exact causal links between internal service quality (e.g., leadership practices, empowerment, and training), employee outcomes (e.g., satisfaction leading to loyalty), external value (e.g., customer's perception of service quality), customer outcomes (e.g., satisfaction leading to loyalty), and organisation performance (e.g., revenue growth and profitability).

MAROUN'S VOICE

If the SPC is put into work:

The logic and the reasoning behind the principles existed within the service-profit chain obviously is understandable and simple; yet, the results of applying them can be extremely powerful.

Simply put, servant leadership enhances the quality of the working environment by providing employees with the skills and empowerment to serve customers and will fuel employee satisfaction.

Satisfied employees become more committed and loyal to the hotel where they are working.

Gradually, over time, those loyal employees acquire all the processes of a quality service and therefore become highly productive.

More employee productivity means improving the external service value in terms of the quality of the customer's experience. Greater quality experience raises customer satisfaction.

Satisfied customers will become loyal customers. Loyalty leads to more frequent visits to the same event or hotel and bigger purchase volumes of their regular and other new products or services.

Overall, this progression eventually results in increasing sales, revenue, and profitability.

References

Greenleaf, R.K. (1980) *The Power of Servant Leadership*. San Francisco, CA: Berrett-Koehler Publishers, Inc.

Heskett, J.L., Jones, T.O., Loveman, G.W., Sasser, W.E. Jnr., and Schlesinger, L.A. (1994) 'Putting the Service-Profit Chain to Work', Reprint 94204, *Harvard Business Review*: Cambridge, MA.

Oliver, R. (1980) 'A Cognitive Model of the Antecedents and Consequences of Satisfaction Decisions', *Journal of Marketing Research*, 17(4), pp.460–469. Available at: https://journals.sagepub.com/doi/full/10.1177/002224378001700405 (Accessed: 3 January, 2022).

Chapter **9**

The Importance of Reflection

This chapter addresses the practice of reflection as a strategy to assess performance towards the goals of the business, to understand whether we are on track to meet them and achieve successful outcomes against the objectives we have set.

We point out how learning takes place from reflecting upon the experiences we encounter, which is presented in the model of Kolb's Experiential Learning Cycle.

Section 9.1 views reflection from the customer perspective whereby The Manager 'walks through' the customer service experience to identify how the customer would receive those services.

In Section 9.2, we identify what would make you complain and present the concept of customer service appraisals.

9.0 The Benefit of Reflection

In every aspect of management, it is important to reflect. This can be seen in most management, theoretical, and academic models, such as the one shown in Figure 9.1. Here, we show a continuous flow which indicates that there is no starting point and no stopping point, but a continuous cycle of review, evaluation, assessment, and adjustment.

DOI: 10.4324/9781003154600-10

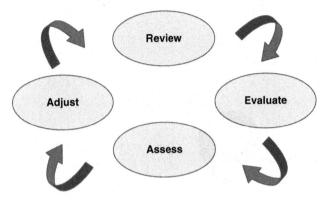

Figure 9.1 Management Model of Reflection

Managing a hotel or an event requires an ability to step back and take a holistic view of what is happening or what is planned to happen.

If reflection is not undertaken, The Manager can become absorbed with the minutiae day-to-day requirements without seeing the bigger picture – seeing only the short-term, rather than the long-term or strategic view. When this happens, the day-to-day way of organising things becomes embedded as the norm, and it will not be considered to change something for the better or identify something which requires changing. We know it as routine or complacency, but it is an approach where The Manager does not stop to take the time to stand back and look at what is happening around them.

Reflection is so important and that is why university degree courses in hospitality management, hotel management, events management, and leisure and tourism management make much effort to provide students with opportunities to develop their reflection skills. Tutors design assessments which include reflective statements, reviews of practical experience, recognition of vocational learning, and reflective reports of a students' placement in industry.

Reflection practice in university courses is not just for fun or to provide the student with variety, it is essential for management students to understand the value of reflective practice and knowing how to perform effective reflection techniques. See Kolb's Experiential Learning Cycle (Kolb, 1984) which is diagrammatised in Figure 9.2.

9.1 Reflecting in the Customer Perspective

The idiom 'the customer is always right' is clearer to interpret when stepping out of the role as a manager and looking at how the customer receives services through 'touch points' (see Martin, 2019).

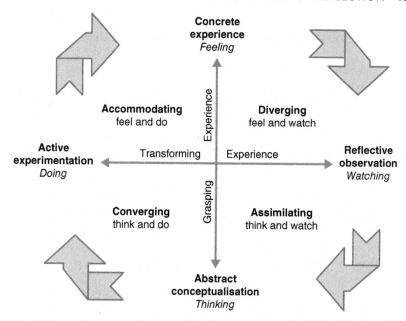

Figure 9.2 Kolb's Experiential Learning Cycle

For a hotel, this may mean The Manager taking time out of the day to check-in as a guest and staying overnight to get the real experience of being a guest and understanding the customer perspective.

Or it could be to take a meal in the restaurant to achieve an understanding of the 'meal experience' which is every detail the customer experiences whilst they are in the restaurant having a meal: the welcome at the restaurant door; the sound level of the music; the comfort of the dining chair; the level of air-conditioning; the position of the table; the speed of service; the noise from the kitchen, etc.

Some hotels provide an overnight stay for their staff either as a perk of the job or as part of their induction as a new member of the team. This helps staff appreciate the customer experience and identify how the customer receives the services at touch points during the customer journey.

Another way for staff to appreciate the customer perspective is by role-plays in one department or across other departments. At reception, for example, staff can take turns in playing the awkward or dissatisfied customer; or a walk-in customer who arrives without any prior booking. Staff can experience what it is like to be a dissatisfied customer whilst training how to deal with a dissatisfied customer.

Role-play across departments allows staff to appreciate how other departments function, the pressures on other departments, and what a customer experiences across other areas of the hotel. Receptionists could inspect bedrooms; chefs could check-in at reception; waiters could clean public areas; etc.

It should be considered that not all staff will enjoy role-play and some might resist working in other departments. Some people are shy or insecure, and this should be taken into account. If a room cleaner in housekeeping is asked to be a waitress to experience another department, she has not chosen the job of a waitress. She might feel happy and secure cleaning rooms but would not be comfortable serving customers in the restaurant.

Events are one-off happenings which a customer experiences at the point of attending the event. When a customer attends, the event is already being consumed at that point so customer service cannot be role-played or corrected, altered or recovered. This means that the customer perspective must be realised before the customer arrives – before the event takes place. Thus, customer service begins with planning the event.

An event organiser can place themselves into the customer perspective by visiting the venue. This alone will identify how easy it is to locate; what signage and directional requirements are necessary for guests to find their way around; entry and exit points; emergency evacuation routes; bottleneck areas such as bars, cloakroom, entrances; visual display opportunities; sightlines to the stage.

When planning the details and content of an event, The Manager needs to reflect how every element will be received by the customer – the customer experience. This extends to the look of the stage for visual impact; the use of special effects to enhance the performance; projection and screens to provide close-up detail for bigger audiences or large venues.

Planning such details includes the marketing which is the beginning of setting customer expectations of the event, the provision of hospitality such as food and drink, comfort such as seating and lounge areas, and opportunities for additional revenue streams which customers might use to enhance their experience such as merchandise.

9.2 Well, Would You Complain?

A hotel manager or event organiser needs to analyse each element of their offering to the customer – what they promise to their customers. Part of the analysis process is to experience what the customer experiences. Whilst doing so through planning, role-play, or testing the experience by oneself, the question should be asked 'would I complain?'

AUTHOR'S VOICE

When designing events, it is usual to consider the customer perspective because events are designed for people to enjoy or have a good time. But it must be done consciously, not subliminally or by routine.

I use the function sheet for this purpose. By constructing the function sheet at the start of the planning phase, I build a feel of how the event will be received by customers. I can track with my eye how a customer will walk through the event and what they will engage with at each touch point.

I use the function sheet to ascertain timings – giving the customer time to access the venue, visit the cloakroom, get a drink, socialise, and relax, and when they will need something to eat.

By putting myself in the perspective of a customer at the event, I can look at the function sheet and 'walk through' the event to see what I would not like about it. Maybe one part is too rushed because I have not allocated enough time, or I might want something to eat at that point, or it is a long wait before the next activity happens, or I would like a break because the session is too long.

AUTHOR'S VOICE

I attended a small conference where guests were served alcoholic welcome cocktails on arrival before the conference began: a nice touch.

Once we were seated for the conference, the audience fell asleep because the alcohol took effect.

The Manager had not considered the customer perspective to offer canapés with the welcome cocktails to absorb the alcohol and energise the audience.

Some venues include that question on an appraisal questionnaire of the service they provide to customers, such as in the example shown in Figure 9.3.

This type of appraisal of customer services can be conducted periodically if it is a hotel, such as weekly or monthly. In which case, there would be a new appraisal form per week.

Service being appraised	Quality 1 (poor) 5 (excellent)	Would I complain?	Notes	Date / Appraised by
Guest check-in	4	No	Required quicker acknowledgement	8th July / Philip Berners
VIP entry	5	No	Quick and efficient process	8th July / Philip Berners
Bar service	2	Yes	Nobody behind bar to serve	9th July / Adrian Martin

Figure 9.3 Customer Service Appraisal

If it is a regular appraisal for consistent service levels, it could be carried out daily or for each service (breakfast, lunch, afternoon tea, dinner). This would be part of the close-down procedures so that an appraisal of service is conducted at the end of each service.

The appraisal form can also be part-completed as a template document for repeat appraisal, so if it was being conducted for each service, there could be an appraisal form for each service time, such as lunch, with standard areas to appraise (Figure 9.4).

Analysing service appraisal forms will identify patterns and suggest where areas are failing and need improving. Over time (hopefully a very short period) the appraisal forms should show a pattern of improvement in quality and service levels.

With events, appraisal can be conducted during the event using a checklist. Some event organisers use the function sheet as a checklist because it already exists and lists each activity that is happening, when it should happen, and who is responsible for it.

A column can be added for The Manager to make notes, and another column can be added for checking (Figure 9.5).

It can be seen in the below example of an event function sheet how each activity can be checked and commented upon so that the organiser has a checklist to reflect how the event ran according to what was planned on the function sheet.

Lunch service	Day	Quality 1 (poor) 5 (excellent)	Would I complain?	Notes
Greeted quickly				
Seated quickly				
Drinks order				
Food order				
Drinks service				
Bill delivery				

Figure 9.4 Service Appraisal Template

Timing	Activity	Responsibility	Notes	Checked
16:00 – 17:00	Rehearsal	Production crew	No issues. On time.	Yes
17:30 – 17:45	All-staff briefing	Phil / All staff	Over-ran 10mins	Yes
17:50	Final walk-round	Phil	Late 5 mins	Yes
18:00	Doors open	All	Late 5 mins	Yes
18:00	Cloakroom open	Cloakroom	No issues	Yes
18:00	Bars open	Bars	No issues	Yes
18:10	Check front door	Phil	Good flow	Yes
18:15	Check chef	Phil / Chef	Ready	Yes
18:30	Serve canapes	Chef / Waiters	Good flow	Yes

Figure 9.5 Event Function Sheet

At the end of the event, all areas would have been checked with a tick in the right-hand column.

This type of appraisal at events is valuable for post-event evaluation and debriefs because the organiser can recall what happened during the event and know that each element of the event had been checked.

If a complaint is received, The Manager can refer to the function sheet and see the comments to identify if the complaint is legitimate.

It is important for The Manager to keep a checklist with notes to refresh the memory because usually complaints are received after the event has finished. Sometimes they are received some days later. Of course, The Manager will not know what complaint is coming in! Events are fast-paced environments and there will be many things occurring during a short time, so to have notes to refer to is extremely helpful.

The purpose of reflection is to appraise customer service so that improvements can be made, lessons can be learnt, and the customer receives a high level of customer service.

INDUSTRY VOICE

'Go the extra mile in customer service'

"In training, your manager will highlight the importance of customer service and how important it is to 'go the extra mile'. But during a long and busy shift, it can be easily get forgotten.

One day, my shift started, and I was immediately very occupied. On top of being busy and serving very discerning guests, one of my customers asked me to do them a favour. He wanted me to collect his new purchase from the men's personal tailoring department located on another side of Harrods.

Well, Harrods is the biggest independent department store in the world with over 1 million square feet of retail space. Across seven floors, there are 330 departments, over 20 restaurants, and tea and coffee shops. For me to walk from my department to the tailoring department would take over ten minutes each way.

Knowing that I could not leave my busy department for that much time, I forfeited my entire break to go and collect my customer's purchase.

I did not have to do it. But, I did choose to go the extra mile for my customer. I decided to use my free time proving how much I enjoy working in hospitality and delivering customer service – not only to my managers and my customer but also more importantly to myself.

My customer was delighted and very appreciative. He gave me a generous tip which I did share with my colleagues, and I proved to be someone who cares."

Olaf Olenski, Customer Service Expert, formerly at Harrods of Knightsbridge, London

References

Kolb, D.A. (2015) *Experiential Learning, Experience as the Source of Learning and Development*, 2nd Ed. Upper Saddle River, NJ: Pearson Education Inc.

Martin, A. (2020) *The Practical Guide to Understanding and Raising Hotel Profitability*. London: Routledge.

Index

Note: **Bold** numbers refer to tables and *Italic* page numbers refer to figures.

accreditation 42, 77, 80
aggressive complainers 127
Automobile Association (AA) star rating 78, 79
awards and accreditations 42

behavioural segmentation 56
brand reputation 14, 15
budget hotel 74

communication process: Cutlip & Center's 7 Cs of effective communication *113*, 113–115; event interdepartmental communication 118; feedback 112; hotel interdepartmental communication 115–116; hotel interdepartmental consistent performance 116–118; interdepartmental communication 121, 122; learning models 114; noise 112, 115; onsite staff briefings 119–121; pre-event briefings 119; project/production meetings 119; Shannon & Weaver model 111, *111*
competition: competitor analysis scatter graph *54*, 54–55; equivalent

product 53; negative feedback 55; quality *vs.* price 53
complaints 123; aggressive complainers 127; apologise 134; attention to customer 133; busy/noisy environment 133; comfortable customer 132–133; complimentary items 135; customer feedback 125, 134–137; dissatisfaction 124; eight-step method 132–137; at events 137–138; Guest response procedure 136; key questions 133; legislation 125–126; legitimate 129–132; levels 147, 148; liability 133; negotiation stages 138–140; outcomes 140, **141**; professional complainer 126; prolific complainer 126–127; resolution options 134; shy complainer 127; transactional analysis (*see* transactional analysis); types 126–127;
contemporary management models 103
contracts: business transaction 90; exchange 93, 94; expectations 93–96; issues 90–91; promises 89–90; schedules 96; suppliers and

contractors 95; value of 91–93; venue choice 95

CRM systems *see* Customer Relationship Management (CRM) systems

customer Balanced Scorecard 28–29, *29*

customer dissatisfaction 72, 148–149; customer experience 49; financial cost 50, 51; lost profit 51; marketing and promotion activities 51; short-term 49

customer expectations 3, 6, 8, 10, *11*, 12–14, 65, 80, 81; honest 70, 71; quality 10, *11*; standards 71–74

customer experiences 168; hearing 82; meal experience 167; sight 82; smell 83; taste 82; touch 83

'the customer is always right' 65; customer service 67; expectations 66

customer journey 41, 43; customer types 16; diversity 16; event night 15; hotel types 16; stakeholder groups 16, 17; touch points 3 (*see also* touch points)

customer loyalty 61–62, 97; leadership level 101–105; management level 105–107; operational level 107–111; repeat customers 98–101

customer misperception 77

customer perception 65–66, 80; accreditation 80; budget hotel 74; five-star luxury hotel 74; hotel brands 75–77; hotel marketing consortia 77–78; hotel style 74; online booking sites 78–80; OTAs 78–80; pricing parameters 74–75; review sites 78–80; star rating 78

customer persona 52

customer perspective 8, 9; Balanced Scorecard 28, *29*; reflection practice 166–169

customer referrals 62–64, *63*

Customer Relationship Management (CRM) systems 52, 60–61

customer service 3, 9, 172; appraisal 169, *170*; benefits 146–149; broken promises 90; business benefits 153–155; consistent 38–41; customer dissatisfaction 148–149; customer benefits 151–153; customer survey feedback questionnaires 4; decision-making 5; employee-centric business 6; event experience 6; financial and social impacts 5; happy customers 98; inconvenience/disappointment 5; leadership level, customer loyalty 102; management benefits 150–151; The Manager 5, 7; post-purchase behaviour 5; quality 41; quality of 6; return customers 31, 34; skills 40; social media 4; staff benefits 150; staff empowerment 147; TQM 26

customer survey feedback questionnaires 4

Cutlip & Center's 7 Cs of effective communication *113*, 113–115

'delight' customers 12

departmental communication 122

Direct-message (DM) customers 39

Electronic Word of Mouth (EWORM) 66, 79–80

employee-centric business 6

employee satisfaction 159–160

error-finding exercise 21–23

error rate, touch points 19–20, *21*

event function sheet 170, *171*

event interdepartmental communication 118

event marketing 82

event objectives: after-event evaluation 85, 86; charity funds 84, 85; customer service 87; KPIs 86–88; performance tracking 86; purposes 84; quantitative/statistical element 86

event planning 82

exit interviews 45

experience economy 82
external communications 14

feedback and evaluation: on booking
    confirmation 39; consistent
    customer service 38–41; consistent
    quality 38; customer service
    skills 40; DM customers 39;
    email surveys, new customers 39;
    informal 34, 35; KPIs 39; link/
    QR code survey, social media 38;
    live process creation 38; on lost
    booking 39; online community
    39; poor planning 35–38; prize,
    for survey 38; procedure 37–38;
    solutions 40; structured 35
fictional customer persona 56, 56
financial perspective, Balanced
    Scorecard 28, 29
five-star luxury hotel 74

Gales, Jean-Marc 17
Greenleaf, R.K. 156
Guest response procedure 136

happy customers: after-event
    procedures 99; business success
    101, 101; customer service 98;
    event organisers 99; feedback and
    evaluation 99, 100; guarantee
    sales 100
Heskett, J.L. 162
hotel architects 83–84
hotel interdepartmental
    communication 115–116
hotel interdepartmental consistent
    performance 116–118
hotel marketing consortia
    77–78
hotel room price 12

InterContinental Hotel Group
    (IHG) 75
interdepartmental benchmarking 117
interdepartmental communication
    121, 122
inter-department social events 115

internal process perspective, Balanced
    Scorecard 28, 29
invitation type 80

Kaplan, R.S. 28
Key Performance Indicators (KPIs) 39,
    86–88
Kolb's Experiential Learning Cycle
    165, 166, 167

leadership level, customer loyalty:
    anonymous feedback 105;
    appraisals 104; contemporary
    management models 103; customer
    service 102; happy staff 101, 102,
    103; hierarchical socio-professional
    structure 102; open-door policy
    105; regular meetings 105;
    responsibility 102; rewards and
    incentives 104
lead-in, pre-event planning 119
learning/growth perspective, Balanced
    Scorecard 28, 29
legislation 125–126
legitimate complaints: client debrief
    meetings 130; compromise/
    goodwill 132; management failure
    131–132; social function 129;
    touch point 130

management level, customer loyalty
    105–107
management model 165, 166
marketing costs 77
member hotels 77

negotiation stages, complaints:
    bargain 139; execute 139–140;
    information 139; preparation
    138–139; summarise 139
noise 112, 115
Norton, D.P. 28

offer to customers: after the event 70;
    ambience 68–69; décor 68; event
    content 70; event purpose 70;
    expectations level 69; facilities 69;

hospitality services 69; marketing 70; pre-event planning stage 70; quality 68; service 68

Oliver, R. 160

online booking sites 78–80

online reviews 14

online travel agents (OTAs) 62, 78–80

onsite staff briefings 119–121

operational level, customer loyalty: responsibilities 108; social merits 107; staff achievements 107–109; underperforming staff 109–111

overselling: customer expectations 10, *11*; customer perspective 8, 9; dishonesty 8; financial sales targets 7; honesty 7–8; limitations 8; The Manager 7; marketing department 9; quality fluctuation 9, *10*; quality line flattening 9, *10*; quality upwards 11, *11*

perception 14

personalised products 57, 59

personalising offer, customer attraction 57–60

personalising sponsors' packages 59

personas creation 57

post-event evaluation and debriefs 171

post-purchase behaviour 5

post-stay customer engagement 37

pre-event briefings 119

prevent/obstruct communication 107

previous experience, customer 14

professional complainer 126

professionalism 41–43, 90, 106

project/production meetings 119

prolific complainer 126–127

psychology 14

quality fluctuation 9, *10*

quality line flattening 9, *10*

quality management 118

quality of service 36

reflection practice 165; appraisal template 170, *171*; benefit 165–166; customer perspective 166–169; customer service appraisal 169, *170*; event function sheet 170, *171*; Kolb's Experiential Learning Cycle 165, 166, *167*

repeat customers 61, 62; happy customers 98–101, *101*; social network 98; *see also* reputation

reputation 80; annual music festival 44; damaged 45; employer/employee relationship 45; event legacy 43; exit interviews 45; long-term sustainability 43; professional 43; service quality 47; supplier quality 48; venue 48

return customers 30; complaints 34; customer details 33, 34; customer service 31, 34; evaluation activities 35; feedback (*see* feedback and evaluation); happy customers 31; and new customers 31; phone enquiries 32, 33

review sites 78–80

Seaview Hotel 75–76

self-development 13

servant leadership *158*; business philosophy 158–159; characteristics 156; concept of 156; customer satisfaction 160–162; decision-making 156; employee satisfaction 159–160; SPC model *162*, 162–163; style 155, 157–158; traditional hierarchy challenges 156–157, *157*; verbal and non-verbal communication 161

service-profit chain (SPC) model *162*, 162–163

service quality management (SERVQUAL) model 27–28, *28*

Service Recovery 23

Shannon & Weaver model 111, *111*

shy complainer 127

social media 4, 14, 49, 72, 73; link/QR code survey 38

socio-professional structure networks 43

socio-structural culture 115
staff empowerment 150, 153
stakeholder groups 3, 16, 17, 36, 45, 76
stock management 21

target market 2, 16, 48, 52; behavioural segmentation 56; customers type 55–56; fictional customer persona 56, 56; personas creation 57; socio-economic banding 56
total quality management (TQM) 3; customer at buffet 27; customer service 26; during-event 24; events management 24; fire alarm system 26; The Manager 23; post-event 24; pre-event 24;

preventative maintenance schedule 25–26; Service Recovery 23
touch points 3, 166; comedy show with meal 18–19; cost implications 22; error-finding exercise 21–23; error rate 19–20, 21; one-off entertainment event 17, 18; 'RAG' rate 22; staff feedback revisit 20, **20**
transactional analysis: adult state 128; advantage 127–128; calming customers 129; child state 128; matching series 128, 128; parent state 128
Tripadvisor 53

underselling 12, 14

word of mouth (WOM) 14

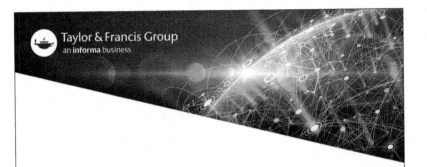